THE REMINISCENCES OF
Captain Winifred Quick Collins
U.S. Navy (Retired)

INTERVIEWED BY
Paul Stillwell

U.S. Naval Institute • Annapolis, Maryland

Copyright © 2013

Preface

This oral history covers the life and career of a U.S. Navy pioneer. She appears in the work with three different surnames: Redden, her birth name; Quick, the name of her first husband and that which she used throughout nearly all of her active naval service; and Collins, the name of second husband.

As Winifred Quick she was one of the first women chosen for officer training when Congress authorized the creation of the WAVES in 1942. She then supervised officer training before being assigned in 1944 to Hawaii, the first of the WAVES to serve in an overseas billet. In 1948 she was one of the first eight women to be commissioned as officers in the regular Navy. From 1957 to 1962 she was the only female line captain as she served as Assistant Chief of Naval Personnel for Women, the top of her profession. In that assignment she pushed for and achieved many advances on behalf of her fellow Navy women.

On the way to that success, she demonstrated an amazing amount of resilience and drive in surmounting the obstacles that came from being part of a broken home. Throughout the reading of her descriptions, one is impressed by the ways in which her vision and charm helped transform situations for the better and create new opportunities. She was proactive throughout, especially in trying to deal with the obstacles thrown in her path by Navy men who were not comfortable serving with women and knew very little about their capabilities. She and thousands of other WAVES won over the reluctant males by their competences and contributions. Around the same time I interviewed Captain Collins, I was also interviewing the first African American naval officers, the Golden Thirteen. I was often struck by the parallels between the discrimination and hostility both the women and the black officers encountered in helping to transform the naval profession.

I greatly regret that it has taken so long for this transcript to become publicly available. Because of competing priorities and changing circumstances, other oral histories moved ahead of it in line. In working with the raw transcript, I have done some editing for the sake of clarity and accuracy, fact checking, annotation with footnotes, and indexing. I take satisfaction that Captain Collins included part of this oral history in a memoir published two years before her death: *More Than a Uniform: a Navy Woman in a Navy Man's World* (Denton: University of Texas Press, 1997). However, many of the names and anecdotes in the oral history did not make it into the book, so there is fresh information here. A further source on her life and career can be found in her collected papers, which are archived in the Schlesinger Library, Radcliffe Institute for Advanced Study, Harvard University, Cambridge, Massachusetts.

As the project finally comes to a close, making available the work that Captain Collins intended for publication, I thank Janis Jorgensen of the Naval Institute staff who coordinated the printing and binding of the finished history.

In completing the volume, the Naval Institute expresses its gratitude to the Tawani Foundation and the Pritzker Military Library of Chicago for their generous financial support of the oral history program that produced this memoir.

Paul Stillwell
U.S. Naval Institute
December 2013

Authorization

The U.S. Naval Institute is hereby authorized to make available to individuals, libraries, and other repositories of its choosing the transcripts of two oral history interviews concerning the life and career of the undersigned. The interviews were recorded on 29 October 1986 and 5 November 1986 in collaboration with Paul Stillwell for the U.S. Naval Institute.

The undersigned does hereby release and assign to the U.S. Naval Institute all right, title, restrictions, and interest in the interviews. The copyright in both the oral and transcribed versions shall be the sole property of the U.S. Naval Institute. The tape recordings of the interviews are and will remain the property of the U.S. Naval Institute.

Signed and sealed this 12/15 day of December 1992.

Winifred Quick Collins
Captain Winifred Quick Collins, USN (Ret.)

CAPTAIN WINIFRED QUICK COLLINS
UNITED STATES NAVY (RETIRED)

Commissioned an ensign in August 1942, Winifred Quick was in the first group of women officers to enter the U.S. Naval Reserve. In September 1942 she was assigned as the personnel director, Midshipman School, Smith College, Northampton, Massachusetts. In this capacity she developed procedures for the personnel classification of 6,000 women officer candidates who reported during the ensuing year. Subsequent Navy assignments included personnel and management billets on a variety of staffs within the United States and overseas; member of the Navy Department Management Team; Division of Officer Personnel, Bureau of Naval Personnel; 12th Naval District Commandant's staff in San Francisco; secretary of the staff of Commander in Chief U.S. Naval Forces Eastern Atlantic and Mediterranean in London.

In 1948, Lieutenant Quick was selected as one of 500 women to be commissioned in the regular Navy. On 9 August 1957 she became the Assistant Chief of Naval Personnel for Women. In this assignment she was the senior woman officer in the U.S. Navy and the only woman line officer serving in the rank of captain. At the conclusion of five years in this billet and 20 years of active naval service, she voluntarily retired in August 1962.

Born: 26 November 1911 in Great Falls, Montana, as Winifred Mary Redden
Married: Roy Quick in 1935, later divorced
Married: Rear Admiral Howard L. Collins, USN (Ret.), in 1961; he died in 1984.
Died: 5 May 1999

Education: University of Southern California, B.S. in business administration, 1930-35
    Radcliffe College (Harvard-Radcliffe Graduate Program in Administration, Certificate, 1937-38
    Stanford University, M.A. in education, 1951-52

Dates of Rank:

Ensign: 28 August 1942
Lieutenant (junior grade): 1 July 1943
Lieutenant: 1 October 1944
Lieutenant Commander: 1 January 1949
Commander: 1 July 1953
Captain: 9 August 1957

Chronological Record of Commissioned Service:

1942-1943   Personnel director for officer training at Smith College and Mount Holyoke

1943-1944	Bureau of Naval Personnel, special assistant on the WAVES planning and management
1944-1946	14th Naval District staff, Pearl Harbor, district personnel officer for the women's reserve
1946-1950	Bureau of Naval Personnel, planning for transfer of women to the regular Navy and establishment of promotion and rotation policies
1950-1951	Staff of the Secretary of Defense
1951-1952	Graduate student, Stanford University, Palo Alto, California
1952-1956	12th Naval District staff, San Francisco, California, assistant director of personnel/director of personnel,
1956-1957	Staff of Commander in Chief Naval Forces, Eastern Atlantic and Mediterranean, London, England
1957-1962	Assistant Chief of Naval Personnel for Women, Arlington, Virginia
1 Sep 1962	Transferred to the retired list of the U.S. Navy

Military Awards:

Legion of Merit
Bronze Star Medal
Secretary of the Navy Commendation Medal
American Campaign Medal
Asiatic-Pacific Campaign Medal
World War II Victory Medal
National Defense Medal

Civilian Awards:

1971 – Secretary of the Navy's Distinguished Civilian Public Service Award

1973 – Navy League Distinguished Service Award

1990 – Inducted into the National Navy League Hall of Fame

1994 – Nominated to the International Hall of Fame of Professional and Business Women

Post-Navy Experience:

National Vice President of the Navy League
National Director and Chairman of the awards committee of the Navy League
National Director of The Retired Officers Association
Director of the Women's Life Insurance Company of America
Consultant to the Department of Health, Education and Welfare
Trustee of the Helping Hand Foundation that aided Vietnamese Navy families
Member of the Secretary of the Navy's Board of Advisors
First Vice President of the Republican Women of the District of Columbia
Director of the Harvard Graduate Business School Club of Washington, D.C.
First woman Director of CPC International, a family of consumer and industrial food businesses
Trustee of the United States Naval Academy Foundation

Interview Number 1 with Captain Winifred Quick Collins, U.S. Navy (Retired)
Place: Captain Collins's apartment, Washington, D.C.
Date: Wednesday, 29 October 1986
Interviewer: Paul Stillwell

Paul Stillwell: Using our customary format, I'd like to start off with when and where you were born and something about your parents and childhood.

Captain Collins: I was born in Montana, and my parents were divorced.[*] I guess from age 13 on, I was pretty much on my own. I lived with relatives a little while, but I really worked my way through in the last two years of high school. After graduation, I stayed out a year and worked to save money for college. Then I went to USC, where I won a scholarship, which paid for part of the cost.[†] I also worked my way through there. I got a job with a very large wholesale pharmaceutical chain.

Paul Stillwell: What year did you enter Southern Cal?

Captain Collins: I entered in '30. Then I stayed out of school another year, my freshman to sophomore, to work to get money. I graduated in 1935.

Paul Stillwell: Did you have a career objective at that point?

Captain Collins: Yes, business and art. That's an odd combination, but those are two of the things I like very much.

Paul Stillwell: How much direction or support had you gotten from your parents toward this?

---

[*] Winifred Mary Redden was born 26 November 1911 in Great Falls, Montana. Her parents were Daniel A. Redden and Mary Winifred Redden.
[†] USC – University of Southern California.

Captain Collins: None at all. I had quite a bit of support from professors, which was very helpful to me, and one in particular became a real inspiration, or a role model, as we say now.

Paul Stillwell: Who was that?

Captain Collins: It was Ada Holmes. She was a professor in business administration, now deceased.

Paul Stillwell: Business was an unusual career choice for a woman at that point, wasn't it?

Captain Collins: I guess so, but I used to read the stock market charts when I was about 12 or 13. My father was a very successful businessman, and I think perhaps that influenced me. He'd keep in touch with me by letters, but I really never lived with my parents after I was 13.

Paul Stillwell: Didn't you go to the custody of either one then?

Captain Collins: Theoretically, I was in the custody of my mother, but that was an unhappy situation for me. So I just went away and worked for my board and room in high school. There was no objection from her.

My father always kept very close in touch. He was a self-educated man but well read, and he was a very staunch Democrat. In his later years, I used to think up things to bug him about the Democratic Party. He'd go down and really do a research paper on it and send it to me. So that was good for him, because he needed that kind of mental stimulation.

Paul Stillwell: What business was he in?

Captain Collins: In Montana he was in mining and the hotel business and just about everything, because that was sort of a pioneer area. He used to tell me that when I was about three he'd bring me a little beer in one of those tiny little mugs and he'd say, "I want to salute you, because if I hadn't run away from home, I never would have met you." He was born in England, and his parents wanted him to be a priest. So he ran away to Canada, and then he came down to Montana. I always sort of prized that precious little story. I guess I was very fond of him because he was encouraging to me in whatever I did career-wise. There was never any doubt, he said, that I was going to go into a career and be a success in it.

Paul Stillwell: Where did you live after your parents broke up?

Captain Collins: I lived first in Montana. Then I went to live with a sister for a brief time in Iowa, and later I came back to Seattle, where my mother and my older brother were living.* He was working his way through college, so there wasn't any support from him, except conversationally we were very friendly. Then I just went out and worked for my board and room. For instance, I'd stay and take care of a youngster and that kind of thing.

Paul Stillwell: Were there any other jobs that you had?

Captain Collins: No, I was pretty busy with high school. I graduated from Broadway High in Seattle, having transferred there the last six months. I took the exams, and somehow I passed. I don't know how, because I'd had such a mixed-up high school.

Paul Stillwell: Where was the bulk of your high school experience.

Captain Collins: One year was at an academy, a Catholic school in Missoula, Montana. The second year, I went with my sister in Des Moines, Iowa. I had two years there, part of it with her and part of it on my own. Then I went back to Seattle midterm and finished

---

* Her sister Evelyn was seven years older than Winifred; brother Dan was five years older.

my senior year there. After that I went to work to get money for college. I don't know why I was so motivated towards college. It never occurred to me I wouldn't go. It's tough for a young man to earn his way, but it was even more difficult for a woman. But there was never any doubt in my mind at all. I never questioned my decision.

Paul Stillwell: That difficulty was compounded by the fact that the Depression had started.[*]

Captain Collins: Oh, definitely, that's right. That's why I had to stay out another year after I started USC, because that was full depression and jobs were very scarce. When I came back, because of this scholarship, the president of this big pharmaceutical company wanted to meet me.[†] He asked me if I would I like a job while I was going to school, and I said I would. So I worked 25 hours a week for $50.00 a month, which is incredible. That came to 100 hours for $50.00. But I was very grateful to have it, because there were so few jobs for students and even full-time people.

That led to a very interesting time for me, because when I graduated, the president of the company said, "Would you like to come and work here?" They had some 600 employees. Some were factory workers in terms of the pharmaceutical side of it. Not having another offer, I said yes. So he said, "What would you like to be?"

I said, "I want to be personnel director." So I went to this favorite professor of mine, Ada Holmes, which was fine with the president of the company. With her help, I did a job analysis of all the different classifications of employees. Then I took it to the president, and I said, "Now, we have to have some increases in salaries, because you have people way down here doing the same as these up here at quite a difference in money."

He said, "I can't do that. I can't raise anyone." He was a multimillionaire, but, I tell you, very tight on the money. Finally, though, he agreed because he liked me, and

---

[*] Following the crash of the New York Stock Exchange in late October 1929, the United States was plunged into the Great Depression, from which it did not recover until the nation geared up for World War II at the beginning of the 1940s. The Depression was marked by high unemployment and many business failures.
[†] Her benefactor was Lucien Napoleon Brunswig, president of the Brunswig Drug Company. He donated the School of Pharmacy at the University of Southern California.

because I argued with him. I said, "This is going to mean the greatest promotion in terms of their work for you if you go down and talk to them about this new plan and tell them what you have in mind." Some of them had never had a raise since they'd been there. What I was proposing were pittance raises in those days, but they were very meaningful to the workers.

Paul Stillwell: The raises were symbolic.

Captain Collins: Oh, very much. And before that, he had never talked to them as a group—ever. So that kind of appealed to his ego, and he went down. Actually, it wasn't costing him a lot of money at all, overall. But these poor factory workers, I just felt so sorry, because there was no plan at all. If one of them gave him a smile, she might get a raise, while someone right beside her, who maybe had three or four kids, would not. The president finally went along with this idea. Professor Holmes was exceedingly pleased with the results and what happened.

About that same time, President Comstock of Radcliffe very much wished to have a management course set up for women.* The idea was to select five women from across the country and have them come to Radcliffe and be taught by Harvard business professors. In those days, we could not enter Harvard Business School itself. That was verboten. So I was selected as one of them, and it was a tremendous experience. We were there one year, but what we had were the top professors, and we did get acquainted with them on a very close, personal basis. They became our friends from then on, after we finished, and followed our careers very closely. It was a most unusual experience.†

Paul Stillwell: So you had the benefit of being in the Harvard Business School, even if not physically.

---

* Ada Louise Comstock served as the president of Radcliffe College in Cambridge, Massachusetts, from 1923 to 1943.
† Shortly after she graduated from USC, Winifred Redden married Roy T. Quick. They separated when she went away to Radcliffe and subsequently divorced. She had the surname Quick throughout her years in the Navy.

Captain Collins: Oh, I think even a greater benefit than being there, because we were the first, and only five. We really had top-notch professors, some of the very famous ones at Harvard business. They took a great interest in this course. One of them, a very famous professor, would be so nervous because of teaching women—and we were right there in the front row—that he'd have to have a martini. His hand would shake when he talked to us.

Paul Stillwell: How sophisticated was business administration education at that time?

Captain Collins: They did have some wonderful time-and-motion studies which one of the professors did, Professor Whitehead.[*] His was the first book that did in-depth study of what motivated employees to work. They found out that the environment, in terms of the interest of the employer, was *the* most important factor. That was the beginning of what we know so much about now. We had him in so many in-depth courses and also consulted with him, so it was a most unusual pioneer atmosphere there.

Paul Stillwell: Was personnel administration a big part of the curriculum?

Captain Collins: Yes, and principally focusing on the management of people. Definitely. The policy of managers, and then the policy of what motivates individuals to produce in the factory, in the office, and in the executive areas. And what makes a team. That kind of thing was included in the early findings from his study at Westinghouse. That was the beginning of behavioral management, you might say. We did the same case studies that they did in the graduate school at Harvard business.

Paul Stillwell: Do you remember any examples of the case studies, or at least the types?

Captain Collins: No, I don't, but they were solutions to business situations—whether it was cost or whether it was a factor of disgruntled employees. The unions at that time

---

[*] Alfred North Whitehead was a British mathematician and philosopher who taught at Harvard from 1924 to 1937.

were quite strong in our country, very strong. The reason the unions grew up was that many of the employers weren't very concerned on how you treat people.

Paul Stillwell: Well, and employers had been forced to pay attention by the Wagner Act, which gave a lot more strength to the union movement.*

Captain Collins: That's right, but I remember Dr. Whitehead telling us some of the experiences he had with employers. They just couldn't believe that it would make a productive difference in their employees by treating them better: painting the walls, showing some attention to them, or giving them a little place where they could have their lunch. That sounds so elementary now in terms of our sophistication, but it wasn't then at all. He would report the difference in productivity, the difference in attitude of the employee toward the employer. It used to be that they were public enemies; one side didn't know anything about the other. The unions, of course, developed that a great deal, I think, in attitude structuring.

Paul Stillwell: There was a time when Frances Perkins, as Secretary of Labor, was very concerned about that.† Was her role discussed?

Captain Collins: We came down to the White House on one of our field trips. We didn't meet her, but we did meet Mrs. Roosevelt.‡ We went to the White House and had tea with her. She was fascinated, of course, with this course, because it was the first in the United States. And she was very gracious. We did meet a tremendous number of top officials at that time. Then we went to New York to some of the top people in retail and wholesale development. We had a very excellent exposure all around, because we were the pioneers in that whole area. They'd never had women in that before.

That was a one-year course, which I finished in '38.

---

* The National Labor Relations Act of 1935 was known informally as the Wagner Act for its sponsor, Senator Robert F. Wagner (Democrat-New York). It created the National Labor Relations Board and established rights of collective bargaining.
† Frances Perkins was Secretary of Labor from 1933 to 1945.
‡ Eleanor Roosevelt, wife of President Franklin D. Roosevelt.

Paul Stillwell: How did you pay for the time at Radcliffe?

Captain Collins: When the president of the pharmaceutical company learned that I had been selected to go to Radcliffe, he was very pleased. He said, "I want to finance you. Why don't I give you $6,000, and if you need more, call me." Considering how I struggled working for him for $50.00 a month, he went overboard. But he was very fond of me, and I think I did some good things for his corporation. He just wrote me out a check. He said, "If that isn't enough, you let me know." I just thought it was like being in heaven to go to school and have all this money. So that was a glorious year for me.

When I came back from Radcliffe, I got a job in Pasadena, California. The state employment agency and the local Pasadena chamber of commerce wanted to get a central place that could assist young people in finding employment. So we set up a counseling service, a testing service, and a placement service, and I was in charge. I always loved something new, and so I had the fun of developing it all. I worked with civic groups, I worked with the top people in the junior college, and I did a fair amount of speaking. I shudder to think how I was then, but I talked a lot of church groups and to chamber of commerce youth groups. And I spoke to groups or associations who were interested in helping young people, because it still was a Depression area in '38.

The young people were having a terrible time, one, finding a job; two, knowing what to hunt for in a job; and, three, what their qualifications were. These were mostly kids who had graduated from two-year junior colleges, but they didn't know where to strike out in their search for employment. So that was part of our program there.

Paul Stillwell: How did you come to that job? Did Radcliffe have a desire to place you specifically?

Captain Collins: Yes, they did, but most of their jobs were in the East. I, being a Californian, felt I had to go back there. I forget just how I heard about this job, but I remember I went over and was interviewed by the superintendent. He noticed my Radcliffe degree, and he said, "Well, I don't want anyone that's been to one of those fine eastern schools. With these kids, I've got to have somebody down to earth. They need to find a job, and they don't know all this eastern stuff."

Then I explained how I'd worked through college, so he appreciated that I had some knowledge of what it was to be hungry and look for a job and all that, which is what those kids were. We became great friends, and I enjoyed the job tremendously because it was innovative. There were no charted courses for me, and that was the fun of it.

Paul Stillwell: Did you keep track in later years of what became of your other four cohorts in that course at Radcliffe?

Captain Collins: Oh, yes, right through the years. We still are very close.

Paul Stillwell: What sorts of things did they go into?

Captain Collins: With the exception of one, they became very high professionally. One who lives here in Washington was an international economist; she stayed another year or so and went on to get her Ph.D at Harvard. Then the second one went to Wellesley and became the personnel director, and she was also very influential in personnel organizations. She is deceased. The third one went into government and became a top personnel director in top government jobs. And the fourth one didn't work. She married, and her husband became an ambassador. They live in Washington too. So we all had rather interesting careers.

When the war was coming on, President Comstock joined the Secretary of the Navy's Advisory Board for Women in the Navy. Because I had been to Radcliffe, she called me from her office in '41 and told me that something very exciting was going to happen in the Navy. She said, "I know it'll just suit you perfectly. Will you go and have an interview?"

I said, "Do they have to wear uniforms?"

She said, "Oh, I don't know that detail," which was definitely a con job.

I said, "Well, I don't want to look like a man and wear a man's tie and all that. And I definitely do not want to be in uniform." But I did go over to look into it. The law was passed July 30, 1942, so I went over, I suppose, in May or June.* There was a tremendous board of people. Only one person there was in uniform. He had a broad stripe, and I didn't know what that was. This board was made up, I think, of deans of local colleges in Los Angeles, because this was a whole new thing, and the Navy was seeking their advice on this. I took part, and it was a very pleasant interview. Afterward someone said, "Would you take a physical?"

I said, "If I take a physical, am I in the Navy?"

They assured me I wasn't, so then I went back for another interview. This time they told me they very much would like to have me in the Navy and added, "What would you like to be?"

I said, "I have no idea. I think you should evaluate me and give me whatever you think I should have." As I told the story years later, I said, "You know, if you're stupid, you end up an ensign." Which is just what I did. The law was passed 30 July, and my commission was dated 4 August. So I was right there at the beginning.

On August 28, the first group of women—which was 120, I believe—arrived at Smith College, which was selected as the indoctrination school for women officers.† We had one month of no indoctrination. We didn't have books. Gene Tunney's muscle builders were sent up there to teach us to march.‡ You can see how unfit that would be, because those men took big steps like that, and we took little steps like this. So they left immediately, and I never learned to march.§ Some people did, but I didn't because some were more interested in it than I was. I would go along when I had to, but I surely never knew how to call orders or turn, left or right.

---

* The WAVES (Women Accepted for Volunteer Emergency Service) were established by law on 30 July 1942. Lieutenant Commander Mildred H. McAfee, USNR, received the first commission in the WAVES and became director on 2 August. Her oral history is in the Naval Institute collection.
† Smith College, Northampton, Massachusetts.
‡ Lieutenant Commander James J. "Gene" Tunney, USNR, had been the heavyweight boxing champion from 1926 to 1928. During World War II, he was in charge of the Navy's program of athletic instruction. The men he recruited as assistants were given direct appointments as chief petty officer specialists.
§ They were replaced as marching instructors by WAVES who had taught physical education as civilians.

Our orders were given by the commanding officer, Captain Underwood, who was selected by Mildred McAfee, then lieutenant commander, Director of Women Accepted for Voluntary Emergency Service.* She really got a prize when she selected him.

Paul Stillwell: Could you describe the training period, please—what you went through there.

Captain Collins: Well, there wasn't any organization. It was too soon. We did have some lectures, and that's about all, but we didn't have textbooks to go with our lectures. So in terms of learning much about the Navy, we learned the history by lecture, we learned some of the protocol by lecture, we learned a little bit about rank. But we really didn't have any concentrated indoctrination at all.

Paul Stillwell: Who were the people giving the lectures?

Captain Collins: Male officers. And even then, it was very limited. Among other things, we had to get the first women uniforms, the first shots, physicals, everything. We were in the structuring process of doing it for the next group that came along.

Paul Stillwell: How capable were the other people who were in the course with you? Did they seem like cream-of-the-crop types.

Captain Collins: Well, they were all highly educated, all of them, very definitely.

Now, if I may, I want to tell you about an experience I had before the Navy. This is how little I knew of it. This was before President Comstock called me.

My young brother had graduated from high school in '41, and I knew he was a highly intelligent young man.† But his grades in high school, like those of a lot of kids, left much to be desired. I said I thought he would have a chance to go to one of the

---

* Captain Herbert W. Underwood, USN (Ret.), had been recalled to active duty for the war.
† Her brother was Lawrence Edward Redden, who was born in 1922, 11 years after Winifred. He was in the Naval Academy class of 1946, which graduated in 1945 because the course was shortened in wartime. He retired from active duty in 1975 as a captain.

military colleges, which I said was far superior to what I had to do, to struggle and work and so forth. I told him, "If you could get an appointment to one of them, I think that would be a thing for you to strive for."

So he came over to Pasadena and lived with me. He went to the first semester of junior college, and he had a part-time job, because we didn't have too much money. I was making $1,800 a year, which is $150.00 a month. It wasn't much to live on, and he didn't do any better. I was pretty upset at that.

I'd heard of a very fine prep school in San Marino, California, which is adjacent to Pasadena. I went down and talked to them. They could take a day student for $50.00 a month. So I took my brother down and had him interviewed and enrolled him. I said, "Now, I'll give you six months, $50.00 a month. After that, if you don't make it, you're on your own."

Paul Stillwell: So that cut your spendable income by a third.

Captain Collins: Quite a bit, yes. But I was very fond of him, and I wanted to help him. They really knew how to how to make him dig, I'll tell you, because he won number one in Southern California.[*]

Then I realized I had to have a congressman, and that was a process I knew nothing about. I did find a Democrat, and he was in Southern California. He came and interviewed me and my brother and recommended him. He had one vacancy. And my brother had passed all the physicals and his final physical. Then he went down to Long Beach Naval Hospital, and the doctor who did his eye examination said his eyes were just absolutely impossible to enter the Naval Academy. That was such a terrible shock. We both cried and were upset. Then I said, "Well, the solution is to go to the best civilian eye man." I made an appointment, we went there, and told him the story. He said, "Your brother's eyes are perfect."

So I said, "Well, what should I do?"

He said, "I'll write a letter to the Navy about it, and I'm not going to charge you a penny."

---

[*] This refers to his standing on a competitive exam to qualify for a service academy appointment.

But I wasn't satisfied yet. I still worried. I wondered what would happen if he went to the Naval Academy and they said his eyes were terrible. I thought he might be sent home. So I called the Naval Academy and asked for the superintendent, Admiral Beardall.* He came to the phone, and I explained I was the sister of this potential midshipman. I said, "I've run into a very difficult problem, and I just want to be sure that I'm doing the right thing by coming to you."

He said, "You had a top civilian eye man in the Los Angeles area?"

I said, "Yes."

He said, "What was the name of this doctor at Long Beach?"

So I told him.

He said, "Well, now, I have to tell you that I would not have the nerve to turn down your brother when you've been such a wonderful sister."

Paul Stillwell: I love that.

Captain Collins: Well, you know, that was my first experience with an admiral, and I didn't really know what an admiral was, to tell you the truth. I'd only seen one, but he was so charming and delightful, it gave me great hope. So my brother went in in June 1942, and I arrived there late August to visit him. He said, "What in the world are you doing here?"

I said, "I'm in the Navy."

He said, "You're in the Navy? What are you?"

I said, "I'm an ensign. That's the lowest rank."

He said, "You're not an ensign. You're God around here."

So we walked around the academy grounds, and he said, "Now, don't hold my hand. I can't sit on the bench. You'll get me in all kinds of trouble, so you watch yourself with me. They won't think you're my sister, and it won't make any difference."

But that was all I knew about the Navy. Now I can go back to getting my orders.

---

* Rear Admiral John R. Beardall, USN, was superintendent of the Naval Academy from January 1942 to August 1945.

Paul Stillwell: How soon did you get your uniforms?

Captain Collins: Within that month. So it was a very busy month. They worked very speedily, because there were 120 of us, and a lot of us going to be retained on the staff. The captain said, "It's all my fault, because I particularly asked for you. Why don't you come over to my office. We'll talk it over." So I went over, and I knew I was in a trap. I didn't know how to get out of it. He explained to me, "I have 500 women officer candidates coming in in ten days. I want you to be the personnel director. You've had a very fine background, and I know nothing about women."

I said, "But, Captain, I know nothing about the Navy."

He said, "That's the beauty of it. We're going to work as a team."

I didn't know that was an unusual situation, an ensign and a captain as a team. So I said, "Could I go and think about this, because I've got to get an organization?"

He said, "I knew you'd say that."

So I went away, and I came back to him. I told him, "This is what I'll need." I want six interviewers, and I want two of them to interview each candidate. Because we have such a short space of time to interview them, in fairness to them, I'd like two opinions. If their opinions don't coincide fairly closely, I will interview them. That way we will give each candidate as much opportunity as we can within the time limit we have."

He thought that was a great idea. So then we worked out the logistics, and I had to design a personnel card and interviewing procedures, etc. It was an extremely busy time, because 500 women did arrive in ten days.

Paul Stillwell: What was the purpose of the interviews?

Captain Collins: To determine their skills and abilities, because how can you place them if you don't know anything about them?

Paul Stillwell: So it was presumed that they would be commissioned?

Captain Collins: There would be eight weeks of training and indoctrination, and then they would be commissioned.

Paul Stillwell: So they weren't getting exactly the program you'd had?

Captain Collins: We had no program, really. They had a full course: books, everything. And it was very concentrated, even in eight weeks, you might understand, to cover the history of the whole thing, ships and aircraft.

Paul Stillwell: Was there some attrition built into the program?

Captain Collins: Yes. I don't think we had anyone fail because of behavioral reason, but academic, we did. Or the individual would request to drop out. Since we were all volunteers, that was a simple matter. Because it was a complete change, strenuous change, for women, and a strenuous change for men, as you well know.

Paul Stillwell: It sounds as if Captain Underwood was making a good-faith effort to make it work.

Captain Collins: Oh, he was tremendous. He'd been retired and then recalled to active duty, but he was superb in his flexibility and adaptability. Mildred McAfee picked him, and they got along very well.

Paul Stillwell: Oh, she picked him, did she?

Captain Collins: Yes. She knew what she wanted for women in the Navy, and she picked top academic women and those with experience. They worked truly very closely.

Every month we had 500 more women candidates come in. You'd just finish one group, and the next morning there would be another 500 on your doorstep. So it was a very intense process we had there.

Paul Stillwell: Did you have any contact with the Army training program to exchange ideas?

Captain Collins: No. The Army women were auxiliaries. So we were the first service to be commissioned. It was sometime after that that the nurses were auxiliaries, too, but we got the law through I believe in '43 to have nurses commissioned with some educational standards. Because many of them were not college graduates at that time.

Paul Stillwell: Before that they'd had essentially relative rank, but not actual rank.

Captain Collins: That's right, relative. That's what the WACs had, and they were a separate corps, whereas we were not a corps at all, as you well know.* We were part of the United States Naval Reserve. We had the same pay and the responsibility as other commissioned officers or enlisted.

Now, the captain called me in after I'd been in that job a while, and he said, "Now, it's a tradition in the United States Navy that we can't have a head of a department the same rank as the subordinates." He said, "I've called Captain McAfee." She made captain in the second year, so that would've been about right, probably the spring. He said, "I recommend you be spot promoted to jaygee."†

So there I was, spot promoted.‡

After I was there a year, I was very disturbed about matching people and jobs. We were doing a fine job of putting down their civilian skills and abilities and their desires, the kind of thing they wanted to go into and so forth, as related to civilian life. But I didn't know anything about the other side. With this civilian skill, where would it fit in? So I talked to the captain, and he called and talked to Mildred on the phone.

---

* Congress created the Women's Army Auxiliary Corps by law, effective 15 May 1942. Congress subsequently converted the group to the Women's Army Corps (WAC), effective 1 July 1943.
† Jaygee – lieutenant (junior grade). Her promotion came in November 1942, three months after she had been commissioned as an ensign.
‡ A spot promotion occurs when an officer is assigned to a billet that calls for a higher rank than the individual has been promoted to by the regular selection process. The person wears the insignia of the higher rank but does not receive higher pay. If the officer is reassigned to another job before being officially promoted, he or she reverts to the rank held before the spot promotion.

Then she came up, and she said, "You know, I never thought about that. That's an important part." So she said to Captain Underwood, "What do the men do in terms of reservists?" They didn't do anything either. So then I was sent to Washington to be on a team to go around the country to all the shore establishments and evaluate them in terms of civilian skills. That was one of the greatest boons in utilization of manpower, because we had many frustrated, highly qualified people put into jobs that were not at all related to what they knew or what they wished to do. So that was a big step forward.

Paul Stillwell: Were billets designated at that point to be occupied by women?

Captain Collins: They were later, but not then. We didn't know enough. At that point, the speed of the war was such that they were just put in. A tremendous number of women officers went into communications, because that's the only place where they really knew they could put women. They could relate their math and their background a little bit to that. But in other kinds, no.

Then I went back to BuPers, and in 1944 the law was passed which permitted women to go outside the continental limits.[*] Hawaii was selected as the place they would go. Captain McAfee called me, and I was then a lieutenant—I think a legitimate one.[†] I don't think I was spot promoted to that rank. She said, "I want you to be ready to leave in a week to go to Hawaii to prepare and find out the kinds of assignments and so forth for 5,000 women officers and enlisted. So I arrived in Pearl October 30, 1944. It was a tremendous job. The Navy was going to have WAVES on three different islands.

Admiral Nimitz was very much opposed to having women out there, because he said he had enough trouble as it was.[‡] And I would agree that he did, but three days after I arrived there, I got a call from his aide. He said, "The admiral would very much like you to come to luncheon."

---

[*] BuPers – Bureau of Naval Personnel.
[†] She was promoted to lieutenant on 1 October 1944.
[‡] Admiral Chester W. Nimitz, USN, Commander in Chief Pacific Fleet and Pacific Ocean Areas, 1941-45. In December 1944 he was promoted to fleet admiral, a five-star rank.

I said, "Well, I'll have to call you back. I don't know what I should do." So I went to my captain, who was also a Naval Academy recall. He said, "Are you sure that Admiral Nimitz wants you to come to a luncheon?"

I said, "Yes, sir, I heard from his aide, and I said I'd call him back."

Paul Stillwell: Now, who was the captain then?

Captain Collins: Captain Lewis.

Paul Stillwell: What was his job?

Captain Collins: He was director of personnel for the 14th Naval District.

Paul Stillwell: So you were attached to the naval district staff?

Captain Collins: Yes, I was on the headquarters staff, and he said to me, "Well, by all means. You have to go. Call him back and say you'll be very honored to accept." And he said, "I'll get you a sedan and a driver."

I said, "What'll I wear?"

He just roared. He said, "You're in the Navy. You wear that same little uniform you have on."

It was that awful gray seersucker. I don't know if you ever saw it or not. I used to call it the mattress cover, because I detested it.

So the day came, and I went to Admiral Nimitz's quarters. He was up in Makalapa, and I climbed a lot of steps going up there.* I went up, and there were the admiral and the aide. Obviously, I was scared to death, but Admiral Nimitz was so charming and so delightful. He took me in his little den there, and he gave me a memorable poster, which was a cartoon about Navy women before the law was passed. It showed a Helen Hokinson parlor pigeon wearing an old fore-and-aft hat on the forward

---

* Makalapa is the name of the area near Pearl Harbor on the island of Oahu, Hawaii, where Commander in Chief Pacific Fleet maintains his headquarters.

part of a battleship.* So he endorsed that for me, and then I went in, and he had his whole operational staff there. Well, I thought, "I just pray I get through this," because I'd never seen so many high-ranking officers in my life.

Paul Stillwell: You must have been overwhelmed by it.

Captain Collins: I was. I was scared to death, frankly. But Admiral Nimitz was so dear to me, and he, I guess, recognized I was scared. I tried not to show it, obviously, but he introduced me to all of them. Somehow I got through the luncheon all right. Afterward a captain by the name of Collins, who was his operations officer, said he would escort me down the steps to my car.† So I went down, and the Marines saluted me, and I saluted them back. I remember that very distinctly. I got in the car, and I thought, "Well, I guess I did all right."

A week later, they were having a reception in Pearl Harbor for Admiral Nimitz, and I was invited to it. As I went through the line, I went up to him, and he said, "Oh, Lieutenant Quick, you certainly made history."

That made me feel very good. I thought, "Well, I did all right, I guess."

He said, "I must tell you, you're the first lieutenant in the history of the Navy who blew a kiss to the commander in chief and hasn't been court-martialed."

That was his delectable sense of humor. He said, "When Captain Collins came back," he said, "I was laughing and laughing. Did you see what happened?"

"And he said, 'No, I didn't.'"

He said, "Lieutenant Quick blew me a kiss."

I never knew I did it, so that was a surprise.

Paul Stillwell: Was there any substantive discussion at the lunch, or was it mostly small talk?

---

* Helen E. Hokinson was a staff cartoonist for *New Yorker* magazine.
† Captain Howard L. Collins, USN, later her husband.

Captain Collins: I don't even remember. I imagine it was small talk. I have no idea. He probably asked me where the women were going to be assigned, and I did know that pretty well, because I knew the three islands. I hadn't visited a lot of activities. I'd been there only a couple of days, you see. So we probably talked about that, I'm sure, and my vast knowledge was displayed quickly to him. You never met him, did you?

Paul Stillwell: No.

Captain Collins: He had a fantastic facility in just putting you totally at ease, really. Otherwise, I think I probably would have fainted, because it was a big change for me in my limited nautical experience to be confronted with that kind of situation.

Paul Stillwell: Well, the lunch, itself, though, was a way of telling you that he had overcome his reservations.

Captain Collins: Oh, no question. Well, what I was going to tell you what he said when Captain Collins came back. He said, "I told him that you'd blown me a kiss." And he said he told Captain Collins, "You know, things are certainly going to change here in Pearl Harbor, but I kind of like it." Wasn't that precious? That's the way he was. After that he thought the WAVES were great. But he didn't know before that, and I could well understand his reluctance to have women on top of all of his other problems: the Japs and MacArthur and now women.*

Paul Stillwell: Well, it was the unknown probably more than anything else.

Captain Collins: That's right, yes. He became a tremendous supporter, and he and Mildred McAfee became very close personal friends. Later he came back and was in Washington at one of our anniversaries. I think it was the third, when there were some 70,000 women around the Washington Monument, and he was the principal speaker. So

---

* General Douglas MacArthur, USA, was Commander of the Southwest Pacific Area. He and Nimitz had decidedly different strategies for fighting the Pacific war.

he was convinced of the wisdom of it then, but not at first. And I don't blame him. Who was? You know, there were a tremendous number of men in the Navy who were very opposed to it, because it was the unknown. Their attitude was, "We know how to manage men, but we don't know how to manage women. What would we do with them and so forth?"

Paul Stillwell: Did you run up against the reluctant types yourself?

Captain Collins: Yes, thousands of them. And my experience taught me that the commanding officers would be very resistant, and then they would be told they'd have so many. Then, once they had WAVES in their commands, they became knowledgeable about them and got to know them as human beings. Then they wanted more. But it was always that first sense of, "What'll I do with all these women? I don't know how to manage women. What will they do? What kind of work?" And that was it. And I don't blame them a bit, because it was so new. But after that they just wanted more and more, because the enlisted women were topnotch people from across the country. They were topnotch secretaries and stenographers, for instance, and so it was unusual for the Navy to get yeoman with that kind of quality.

Paul Stillwell: Were you doing missionary work going to the various commands?

Captain Collins: Yes, I inspected all the commands, talked to commanding officers. They'd have a staff meeting, and I'd ask them the kinds of skills they wanted for enlisted women and for the women officers, and I'd tell them what was available. Fortunately, I knew quite a bit about the women officers' abilities, because I'd been in on the process for a year. I had processed some 6,000 of them before I left Northampton. The first contingent of 500 arrived either New Year's Day of 1945 or right after that. But it was a fast-moving scenario I had there.

Paul Stillwell: Interestingly, Admiral Nimitz left shortly after that.

Captain Collins: He did. Yes, he moved his headquarters shortly afterwards.* And the Captain Collins that I met that day is the one I later married. He told me later that when he came to Washington, he was walking down Constitution Avenue near the old Navy headquarters, a woman officer saluted him. He said, "I ducked. I was so overcome, I didn't know what to do."

I mentioned my first arrival at Pearl Harbor on October 30. Within the next few days I was invited to a very lovely party. It was a destroyer party, I guess, and the man I sat next to was Admiral Lockwood.† I saw so many senior officers, and I didn't know what their jobs were. I knew their names, but there were so many commands that unless you had a roster before you, you wouldn't know who they were. In making conversation I said, "Sir, are you getting any WAVES?"

He said, "Oh, my God, no. "I'm commander of Submarine Force Pacific."

I said, "Oh, I'm terribly sorry. I just don't know all the commands here. I didn't know you were, and I beg your pardon."

The next day he called me at the office, and he said, "I want you to come over to lunch. I'll send a car for you."

So I went in to my boss, and I said, "Admiral Lockwood wants me to come to lunch."

He said, "I wonder why?"

I said, "I know he's not having any WAVES, that's for sure."

He said, "No, he wouldn't."

It turned out that a successful submarine was coming in, and Admiral Lockwood wanted me to be there for the celebration luncheon.‡ Well, I've never seen anything so exciting. He was just so good to me from then on, all the time. But, you know, like Nimitz, I thought I'd just blown the whole thing. But that was such an exciting experience because I didn't know they did that, and I'd never seen it, obviously. I was

---

* In late January 1945 Fleet Admiral Chester W. Nimitz, USN, moved the Pacific Fleet headquarters from Pearl Harbor to Guam. He took with him only a relatively small staff, leaving the remainder of the staff in Hawaii.
† Vice Admiral Charles A. Lockwood, Jr., USN, served as Commander Submarines Pacific Fleet from February 1943 to December 1945.
‡ The submarine was the USS *Barb* (SS-220), commanded by Commander Eugene B. Fluckey, USN.

able to meet the commanding officer of the submarine, have lunch with the crew, and hear all about their patrol.*

Paul Stillwell: What did your day-to-day-type activities consist of in Pearl after the initial groundbreaking had been done?

Captain Collins: Well, two first-class yeomen followed me out before the 500 arrived, and they were my working hands, you might say.† I'd go to all these activities, find out what they wanted, and then from then on, I would assign the WAVES as new contingents arrived. Then, of course, the war was over in the summer of '45, so we didn't have too long.‡ Then I was retained to work on the demobilization of these women, and I think I was spot promoted to lieutenant commander, which was a big rank then for a woman.

Paul Stillwell: Considering that's what Mildred McAfee started as.

Captain Collins: That's right.

Paul Stillwell: Did you report to her regularly from Pearl?

Captain Collins: Not really, no. I reported right to my boss, a male officer. She was well aware of what was happening. She came out on a couple of visits while I was there, and I explained some of the problems we had. We lived in BOQs.§ Our area was partitioned off from the men, but we had the same kind of living conditions. Then they built a tremendous number of enlisted barracks, and they were surrounded by big fences to protect them from the male animal. But it was a six-day week, so there wasn't too much time off.

I have to tell you about one incident that was very amusing. A multimillionaire businessman from Denver gave the women officers a beautiful home at Kailua. It's

---

* For details see Collins's memoir *More than a Uniform*, pages 82-83.
† Yeoman First Class Mary Iacona, USNR; Yeoman First Class Geraldine Magee, USNR.
‡ The Japanese ended hostilities in the Pacific on 15 August 1945. They formally surrendered on board the battleship *Missouri* (BB-63) on 2 September of that year.
§ BOQ – bachelor officers' quarters.

across the Pali from Pearl Harbor and right on the beach.* It was a gorgeous place. Two of my friends and I went over on a Sunday, which was our only day off, to go swimming and enjoy this beautiful place. It was right on the ocean—a magnificent place and beautifully furnished. He also left us a little Chinese boy and a maid, so it was a great treat to be away from the BOQ and to be out of uniform.

So one day we came back from swimming and went in and showered. I was the first one dressed, and just as I came out in this beautiful living room, I saw the houseboy letting a man in from the beach, which was the front of this house. He was wearing shorts, because he'd been walking and swimming. I recognized the man immediately as Admiral Halsey.† He didn't say who he was, so I just said that I was Winifred Quick. I didn't know what else to do. If he doesn't say he's in the Navy, should I say I'm in the Navy? So I asked him if he'd like a drink. And he said he would. So the houseboy went to get him a drink, and he said, "Well, this is certainly a beautiful place you have here." He said, "Have you lived here long?"

I said, "No, sir."

He said, "Do you expect to stay long?"

I said, "I think quite a while."

So he said, "Are you here alone?"

I said, "No, I'm here with two other friends. You'll meet them in just a few minutes." I think he'd finished his first drink, and then my second friend came out, and I said, "This is my friend Winifred Love," still not saying anything about the Navy, because I thought I would just play it the way he did. Fine, he had a second drink, and then my third friend came out. I said, "This is Louise Wilde."‡

He put down his drink, looked at his watch, and he said, "I have to leave right away." It just seemed like a complete change in him, and he dashed out the door.

The next morning I got a call about 9:00 o'clock. I answered the phone, and I said, "This is Lieutenant Quick."

---

* Nuuanu Pali is a cliff and mountain pass at the head of Nuuanu Valley, about six miles from Honolulu, Hawaii.
† Admiral William F. Halsey, Jr., USN, served as Commander Third Fleet from 15 March 1943 to 22 November 1945.
‡ The two officers, both lieutenants, had been classmates of Quick during the Smith College training.

He said, "This is Admiral Carney. I'm glad you're admitting you're in the Navy."* Then he said, "Do you know who I am?"

I said, "Yes, sir. You're chief of staff to Admiral Halsey."

He said, "Do you know who visited you yesterday?"

I said, "I most certainly do."

He said, "Why didn't you tell him you were in the Navy?"

I said, "He didn't tell me he was in the Navy."

So he said, "Well, I must tell you that the aides in intelligence have had a very interesting night. Admiral Halsey came back, and said, "You won't believe it. There are three spies living up there: Quick, Wilde, and Love." The Third Fleet recreation area for the officers was about a quarter of a mile from us. "He said, I know what they're going to do. They're going to waltz down the beach and get acquainted with our officers. They're going to find out when were leaving, what our next objective is. I can see the whole thing."

So he told the aide to get the intelligence section to find out. So the aide came in the next morning, and Admiral Halsey said, "Well, what's the story?"

He said, "A millionaire Denver man gave it for the use of naval officers."

Halsey said, "I didn't see any naval officers."

The aide said, "Women naval officers, sir."

Admiral Halsey said, "Oh, my God, I've been had."

So after Admiral Carney told me that, I didn't know what kind of trouble we were in. But then Admiral Carney said "Admiral Halsey would like to get better acquainted with the three former spies: Quick, Wilde, and Love. He wants you to come to a brunch. We'll send a car at 11:00 o'clock. Wear your uniforms and bring your bathing suits."

That's a true story. And after that, why, whenever he came back from his missions, he always invited us.

Paul Stillwell: The former spies.

---

* Rear Admiral Robert B. Carney, USN. Later, as a four-star admiral, Carney was Chief of Naval Operations from 1953 to 1955.

Captain Collins: Yes. I was talking to Admiral Carney the other day, and I said, "Do you remember the story of three spies—Quick, Wilde, Love?"

He said, "I'll never forget it."

Paul Stillwell: How was Admiral Halsey after he found out who you were?

Captain Collins: Oh, charming, wonderful, yes. And Admiral Carney had said, "Well, how did you recognize him?"

I said, "With all of his pictures in every news magazine and every newspaper."

He said he couldn't get over it—Quick, Wilde, Love. Halsey said, "I know they're spies. They've got a beautiful home. They have a houseboy. I don't know; he may be Japanese. I couldn't find out how they were earning their money. The whole thing fits in a neat package."

I could see his point of view. He figured the whole thing was a setup, see, and he thought, "Boy, I've got them." But we became great friends after that.

Paul Stillwell: What were some of the difficulties you encountered when the first enlisted women came to Pearl Harbor?

Captain Collins: The main problem was keeping the men away. Basically, that was it.

Paul Stillwell: Where did the women wind up living?

Captain Collins: Do you know Pearl Harbor reasonably well?

Paul Stillwell: No, not too well.

Captain Collins: Their quarters were where the Navy-Marine Corps golf course is now. The CECs constructed barracks and a mess hall for them.*

---

* CECs – officers of the Navy's Civil Engineer Corps, who direct the construction work of the mobile construction battalions (Seabees).

Paul Stillwell: Where did they wind up even before there was that formal an arrangement for them to live?

Captain Collins: Well, these first two that I mentioned arrived in Hawaii in December '44. The only place I could find for them where they could live and have some protection was the dispensary. The commanding officer of the naval air station at Pearl Harbor was Captain Ingalls, who was one of the first naval aviators.[*] He was a great friend, and he said, "I think this is the best place for them." Well, these poor kids were isolated completely. So every day I'd go over and take them somewhere, because their morale was sinking down to here.

Paul Stillwell: So you would, in effect, escort them on liberty?

Captain Collins: As much as I could. I was very busy, you can understand, because I knew the first 500 women were coming the first or second of January. That gave me a very short time to do all the job I had to in terms of finding out what the COs wanted and where the women would go. When the first two enlisted women came, they were a godsend to me in terms of my job, and I would take them out. I remember I took them at Christmas to a beautiful hotel that had a Christmas hula, and they began to really enjoy it out there, which is a beautiful place. But if you have to live enclosed and can't go out anywhere, that's no good. I don't care where you live.

Paul Stillwell: I think we might mention the names of those two for the record: Yeoman First Class Mary Iacona, and Yeoman First Class Geraldine Magee.

Captain Collins: That's right.

Paul Stillwell: Where did they take their meals?

---

[*] Captain David S. Ingalls, USNR. In World War I Ingalls became the Navy's first fighter ace. From 1929 to 1932 he was Assistant Secretary of the Navy for Aeronautics. He was recalled to active duty for World War II.

Captain Collins: At the enlisted mess, which was a terrible thing for them to go through.

Paul Stillwell: Did they get catcalls and so forth?

Captain Collins: I'm sure, terrible, yes. Because, remember in those days there were no restrictions. They could get whistles and catcalls and everything. So it was a depressing emotional experience for them, until the first group arrived in early 1945. Then these two could live with them. But that December was a horrendous experience, just because of the numbers of men there and two women. And there was nothing I could do about giving them any other than going through the regular mess, obviously. But I did compensate to them, because I had a Jeep and we'd go on liberty together. I'd take them around Honolulu; otherwise, they had no way of seeing anything. They became very close to me, as you can understand, and vice versa.

Paul Stillwell: They were like your dependents.

Captain Collins: That's right. I haven't heard from Geraldine Magee for years, but I still hear from Mary Iacona every year. She lives in Massachusetts now. That is a long number of years to keep relationships.

Paul Stillwell: During your working time there in Hawaii, what did you find out about the actual billets and ways the women were being used? Were these things fed back into the training program and into the classification and assignment process?

Captain Collins: Well, by the time I got all of that finished, the war had terminated, and they shut down Smith College. So it was kind of late to get full benefit of that—there's no question. We really just scattered them, and some of them built their own idea of what they should do. That was part of the process of women finding out how they could be useful in the Navy, really. They might be assigned in communications, and they might be assigned in administrative work. Those were really the two main areas. Some went into public relations as assistants.

Paul Stillwell: You talked about the women being walled off from the male animals. Were there rules of conduct set down?

Captain Collins: Oh, definitely. On both sides of the street, yes.

Paul Stillwell: Were infractions dealt with severely?

Captain Collins: Definitely, yes. They had to be.

Paul Stillwell: I would think just the opportunity to be in the islands would be a strong motivator for good conduct, because, presumably, they could be sent away if the weren't well behaved.

Captain Collins: Well, the good conduct on the women was practically 100%. But on the men, it wasn't quite that good. And that was the problem. That's why we had patrols. The men would try to sneak into the women's barracks and all that kind of thing.

I never will forget going into male officers' mess the first day I was there. They practically stared, like great big goggles at me. It was an inhibiting kind of an experience for a woman, because we were so outnumbered that you kind of wanted to cling with women in a sense. And we, of course, set up recreational facilities in which the enlisted women could meet men. And the women officers were certainly free on their own to go to the clubs and so forth, and they had no difficulty meeting men, I assure you. It was a case of fighting them away. But it was a tremendous experience.

Paul Stillwell: Did you feel self-conscious a good deal of the time?

Captain Collins: Well, in the beginning I did, because I was an oddity. The ratio was probably 1,000 to one, or 5,000 to one, probably. So, in that sense, yes, I was very self-conscious. And the other thing, I think, was that I was very self-conscious about making a good impression, doing the proper thing, and knowing what to do. That was part of the problem. I really didn't know how to handle these situations or know what to do as a woman. It was all clear-cut for the males, but as a woman, it was a different cultural system in a sense. For instance, senior officers were supposed to go in the door before you and all these things, so it was difficult to adapt to that culture for many women. There's no question.

Paul Stillwell: And the men probably had some awkwardness in knowing how to react to you.

Captain Collins: That's absolutely right, yes. I remember I was stationed at the Pentagon for a brief time, and somehow my timing would always be such that Omar Bradley and I would arrive at the same time.* He insisted that I go first, although I kept telling him that it was not right. He says, "I'm a general in the Army. You'll have to do what I say." Charming man. Much of the personality of Admiral Nimitz. Very down to earth and very gracious.

I said, "I can't let anyone see this happen."

Paul Stillwell: You mentioned being an oddity. I would think that you had some good background for that in that you'd done unusual things prior to that, particularly the Radcliffe experience, where you were used to being on display.

Captain Collins: Yes, that's right. We were definitely on display. I would say this was a reverse cultural shock to the professors, because they weren't accustomed to teaching women, and they didn't know how to handle it at first, really. As we progressed in the course, we used to just sit around, all of us together, instead of their standing up. Raffelsberger was a very famous professor at Harvard business, and he just got so nervous that his hand would shake the whole time he was giving his lecture.

Paul Stillwell: You spoke about some of the women being in the public relations area. Was there a special effort to give recognition to the jobs women were doing in the Navy?

---

* General Omar N. Bradley, USA, served as Chairman of the Joint Chiefs of Staff from 16 August 1949 to 14 August 1953. In 1950 he was promoted to five-star rank, general of the Army.

Captain Collins: No, not at that point. We were too new. It was really just a "put them in someplace" kind of thing. Of course, the manpower shortage was tremendous. They were pulling the men out all the time. The Navy just kind of tossed these WAVES into jobs, and the women found their way or didn't, if you know what I mean. Because we didn't have the knowledge to know what was needed, and a lot of the commanding officers didn't know a great deal about the shore billets. Let's face it. They knew about running ships, but shore billets were also big in World War II. And a lot of them did not know how to do it and what kinds of skills were needed for many of these shore billets.

Paul Stillwell: Did some of the women in Hawaii wind up being instructors teaching classes to men?

Captain Collins: Yes, they did. A lot of the women officers and enlisted women ended up in teaching others, because we set up enlisted schools immediately. Some of the officers from those classes would go right out to be instructors, or officers in charge, or whatever. There was always a male officer, senior to her, usually a captain. But the WAVES were used immediately in the teaching situation, which was easier to adapt to, because many of them had been in teaching.

Paul Stillwell: Sure.

Captain Collins: So that part of it made great sense. What wasn't easy for them was to adapt to the Navy type of instruction and that type of thing.

When the war ended, we had 86,000 women on active duty, enlisted and officers. Do you want me to go on?

Paul Stillwell: Please.

Captain Collins: I'll try and follow maybe my notes a little bit here.

Then in 1946, I returned to Washington, and I was assigned to the Potomac River Command as the senior woman officer. We still had a number of enlisted and officers on active duty. I was there just a couple of months. By then Mildred McAfee had gone back to Wellesley, and we had an interim captain named Jean Palmer, who was there for about two months.* And Joy Hancock was appointed as the Naval Reserve woman's director.† We were still voluntary, but our numbers were diminishing because of demobilization, of course.

Paul Stillwell: Are there any special experiences you want to discuss in connection with demobilization? What did that process involve for the women?

Captain Collins: Same as the men. We had to go through the same demobilization.

Paul Stillwell: Was there a point system as the men had?‡

Captain Collins: No, no, they didn't have to have a point system. Because the women were volunteers, if they wished to leave they could. That was the simple part of that part, but in terms of the demobilization process, they went right through those central activities that we had. We had a lot of women working in that to assist in that.

Paul Stillwell: Well, it creates a new problem, though. These women have been doing useful, valuable jobs, and if they can leave at will, then you have to find other ways to do those jobs.

Captain Collins: Yes, but a lot of the activities, you see, were closing down tremendously too. I don't think that we had that problem, really, of the women just wishing to leave the way some of the men who had been in so long and away from families. But I don't think we ever prevented a woman, enlisted or officer, from leaving

---

* Captain Jean T. Palmer, USNR, served as Assistant Chief of Naval Personnel for Women in 1946.
† Captain Joy Bright Hancock, USNR, was Assistant Chief of Naval Personnel for Women from 1946 to 1953. Her memoir is *Lady in the Navy: a Personal Reminiscence* (Annapolis: Naval Institute Press, 1972).
‡ For the demobilization of the U.S. armed forces after World War II, the services had a point system to determine individual priorities for leaving the service. Points were awarded for length of service, overseas service, battle stars, decorations, and dependent children. Those with the highest number of points were the earliest discharged.

if she wanted to go. I don't think we held them back. Maybe in some cases we held them back until we could get a replacement, but it was an easy process for them to depart.

Paul Stillwell: What were the logistic aspects of the demobilization of women?

Captain Collins: They went back on planes. When they came out to Pearl some of them came on hospital ships, but I don't think any went back on hospital ships, because they were so filled with casualties.

Paul Stillwell: Probably a lot of repatriated POWs too.[*]

Captain Collins: Yes, I'm sure of that. But, you know, there were so many cargo planes operating. That's the way most went back. The men went back on some carriers, remember, when they slept on the hangar decks. But I think all of our women went back by plane, and we didn't quite get up to the 5,000 we expected. Things were demobilized before the war ended. One very interesting thing, Commodore Perry, who was with the CECs, had built some beautiful quarters in Pearl Harbor across from Makalapa.[†]

Admiral Towers was the commander in chief by then.[‡] His staff offered to give us these quarters. Compared to the BOQ, they were like heaven. They were Quonset huts with two bedrooms, a living room in the middle, and one little mess for meals.[§] I was in charge of that too. I had lots of jobs. But I got a woman attendant up there to really manage it. I also had a chief steward who had been in the Navy 29 years or something, mostly aboard ship. The kitchen facilities and reefer were beautiful because of the CEC. I tried to teach him how to cook frozen things, such as vegetables. He'd cook them an hour, which was far too long. So I had a great diplomatic mission in, one, having him have a woman officer as his boss, and, two, teaching him that we wanted them cooked three minutes. He'd just shake his head.

---

[*] POWs – prisoners of war.
[†] Commodore John R. Perry, Civil Engineer Corps, USN, officer in charge of the Second Naval Construction Brigade.
[‡] Admiral John H. Towers, USN, served as Commander in Chief U.S. Pacific Fleet and Pacific Ocean Areas from 1 February 1946 to 1 January 1947.
[§] A Quonset hut is a semi-cylindrical metal building that can be shipped to an advance base area and erected quickly.

One time, I invited Admiral Towers and some of his immediate staff members, about ten of them, including George Anderson, to come up there for dinner.* Well, I tell you, the chief was just about to be fit, so we went over ten times that we'd have roast beef, how long it was to be cooked, how long the vegetables were to be cooked. I would see him peeking out from the kitchen to see how things were going. Finally I told Admiral Towers about him, and he said, "Well, let me go back and say hello to him." Oh, that was his day. An admiral had never complimented him before, in his whole career, on his cooking.

Also, I had several Filipino enlisted men. Their machetes were very useful instruments. They were really young—19, maybe, or 18. We would get them into the Navy after they'd been fighting the Japs quite a while in the Philippines. They were wonderful, absolutely wonderful. They took care of the quarters. And so that was another interesting side job I had which I enjoyed. It was certainly lovely living. We could have 16 women officers up there to live, two to a room, and oh, it was heaven.

Paul Stillwell: Did you have any impressions of Admiral Towers from that or other meetings.

Captain Collins: Oh, yes. I got to be very well acquainted with him. I used to fly back to Washington frequently when he was coming back. And after the war, I went out to see him when he was still in his quarters.

I have an interesting story to tell about his wife, Pierre.† Admiral Towers was very formal in his interpretation of how he should act, and he didn't convey that too well to his wife. One Sunday morning he was over at the Makalapa headquarters, looking over the dispatches. As he came out, he heard this violent Hawaiian noise up on Makalapa, which was a total disregard of his orders that everything should be quiet. Here his wife had a whole Hawaiian band on the front of their lawn, taking pictures. She was

---

* Captain George W. Anderson, Jr., USN, was then serving as assistant to the Deputy Commander in Chief Pacific Fleet, Vice Admiral John H. Towers, USN. Anderson later became a four-star admiral and served as Chief of Naval Operations from 1961 to 1963.
† His wife was Pierrette Anne Towers.

making a recording for some magazine—I think *Vogue* or something. It was just hysterical.

I had some friends there, the Von Holdts. He was born in Hawaii, and she was head of Red Cross when I went out there. We became very great friends, and they'd often invite me over to their civilian quarters on the other side of the islands for the weekend. They also invited Admiral Blandy and all of the senior officers.[*] So I got to know all the top admirals of the Navy that way, including Admirals Spruance and Towers, very much so.[†] We became close friends, because I went out from Washington to visit them several times when they were still on duty there.

Paul Stillwell: I know his biographer would welcome any vignettes or personality aspects you recall about Admiral Towers.[‡]

Captain Collins: Well, I'll do a little concentration on that. It just occurred to me that one time, about that blast he heard. And she had that music all amplified on top of everything else. He was just infuriated with her, but she went her own way always.

Paul Stillwell: By then had the ground been broken so that women were more accepted than in the beginning?

Captain Collins: Oh, yes, definitely, yes.

I was saying Joy Hancock had been appointed as a captain and head of the WAVES. She wanted me to come over to BuPers, assigned in officer personnel. My job was partly to help with the legislation, but principally to set up the standards for women officer selectees for the regular Navy—in terms of age and qualifications—because we were to have 500.

---

[*] Rear Admiral William H. P. Blandy, USN, was serving in mid-1945 as Commander Cruisers and Destroyers Pacific Fleet. In 1946 he headed the joint task force that conducted atomic bomb tests at Bikini Atoll in the Marshall Islands.
[†] Admiral Raymond A. Spruance, USN, served as Commander in Chief U.S. Pacific Fleet and Pacific Ocean Areas from 24 November 1945 to 1 February 1946.
[‡] Clark G. Reynolds, *Admiral John H. Towers: The Struggle for Naval Air Supremacy*, (Annapolis: Naval Institute Press, 1991).

Paul Stillwell: Had that already been legislated?

Captain Collins: No. And there was tremendous opposition from many sources, civilian as well as military, to having women in the regular Navy: "Why do you need them?" The Navy's philosophy at that point was that it needed women as regulars so they could serve as a nucleus to continue to experiment. That would enable the Navy to know what the women could do so that in time of another war, we would have the basic knowledge for fast expansion. Even at that point we didn't have any idea of the variety of jobs women could hold. As it was, once they got into their jobs, whether communications or whatever, they stayed there. They didn't get any opportunities for further jobs.

Paul Stillwell: I guess the idea was to keep from having to start over again as they had in World War II.*

Captain Collins: That's right, yes. That was the basic philosophy. The enlisted men, both retired and active, were violently opposed to it. The Fleet Reserve did a tremendous amount of lobbying, opposing the legislation.† Somehow, they perceived the women as a threat to them. That was because the enlisted women were beautifully educated—some even had college—in contrast with a lot of the enlisted men at that time. Many had completed only about the tenth grade, and I think a small percentage were high school graduates. Also, many of the senior officers of the Navy were opposed. They didn't see the sense of it.

Paul Stillwell: Did Admiral Nimitz come to your aid in this?‡

Captain Collins: He never had any women actually working on his staff while he was CinCPac, because, as you know, he left Pearl Harbor in January of '45 and moved his headquarters to Guam. And from Guam, he then went back to Washington and became

---
* The Navy had employed women as "yeomanettes" during World War I but then discharged them after the armistice rather than continuing with a cadre of women on active duty.
† The Fleet Reserve Association is an organization that represents retired enlisted personnel.
‡ Fleet Admiral Chester Nimitz, USN, served as Chief of Naval Operations from 15 December 1945 to 15 December 1947.

CNO. There in Washington, he did have women working for him, both officers and enlisted, but that was his first experience. And, yes, he was supportive. I think I probably still have some congressional letters about it. And from many senior officers we had very high support and very good help in trying to get this legislation passed. But it was at that point very controversial. There's no question about it. It wasn't passed until July '48, and so we worked on it for a two-year period before that.

And put together all the statistical information, and, of course, we had to set different, higher ages for the women than for the men who would normally be transferred to the regular Navy, because we wouldn't have any women left if we had the same age. Because these were to be the first women in the regular Navy, those that had been in the reserve should have an opportunity of becoming regular Navy. It was quite a job to put them older than the men, but they couldn't be too old, or they wouldn't have time to serve. We did have some exceptions, such as women lieutenants who were retired because they weren't selected for lieutenant commander, that kind of thing. And they were overage too. So the first women who went into regular Navy were in an older age group,

Paul Stillwell: Then you really would have your pick of the best people in filling those first slots.

Captain Collins: Definitely, definitely. We did. It was a very splendid selection. We had physical standards. I consulted with BuMed and then the educational people.[*] The age was our big problem, but that was finally approved. It took two whole years for legislation, which isn't too bad in terms of how slow that process is, of getting a new law passed.

Paul Stillwell: Do you remember if Carl Vinson took a personal interest in this?[†] He

---

[*] BuMed – The Navy's Bureau of Medicine and Surgery.
[†] Carl Vinson of Georgia entered the House of Representatives in 1913 and was appointed to the Naval Affairs Committee in 1917. He became the ranking Democrat in 1923 and chairman in 1931. When the Armed Services committee was formed in 1947, Vinson became chairman and held that position, except for two short periods when Republicans held the House, until his retirement from Congress in 1965. The aircraft carrier *Carl Vinson* (CVN-70) is named for him.

controlled a great many things.

Captain Collins: Yes, I know he did. I think Admiral Nimitz was instrumental in getting him to help, because Admiral Nimitz was much regarded by Carl Vinson, I know. But I can't remember the details of it. I knew it very well then, but it's a long time ago.

Paul Stillwell: Part of the delay may have been occasioned by the big squabble that was taking place between the services over unification.

Captain Collins: I don't know. That didn't affect us, really. See, this was just a bill for Army, Air Force, and Navy. So all the services were trying to get this passed.

Paul Stillwell: But I'm suggesting that their attention was probably distracted.

Captain Collins: Oh, yes. Legislatively, I'm sure it was, yes. But there was also an awful lot of opposition to it, just plain opposition to having it. So you're right about unification and that happening at that time.

But why would women need to be in the regular Navy, and what would we do with them? Well, that was part of the idea, to find out what we'd do with them. What they could do, really, is what it amounted to. And what kinds of training they should have. After the law was passed, I was with Joy and six others, officers I picked from every branch of the service—Supply Corps, etcetera, and different ranks—to be the first eight women sworn in the regular Navy.

Then I was retained there in officer personnel to set up the procedures for women in terms of careers in the regular Navy. I wrote the letter which dealt with the rotation of women officers. You'd think the sky was going to fall on BuPers. Absolutely. And, you know, as you have to go through the whole place to get all the initials on it, although I wrote it, I didn't admit to it. I said that the Chief of Naval Personnel had directed this, that I was simply following orders, and that women were part of the regular Navy. Congress had decided that. I didn't have anything to do with it. Because they wanted to really beat on me, for sure.

Was this Admiral Sprague at the time?*

Captain Collins: Yes, and he was very much for it.

Paul Stillwell: Were you one of the first eight regular officers?

Captain Collins: Yes.

Paul Stillwell: That's quite an honor.

Captain Collins: I was a lieutenant commander, and then we had others in ranks all the way down. Joy was a captain.†

Paul Stillwell: So were you second in seniority among the group?

Captain Collins: I'd have to check that. I don't remember. I remember I picked them, and I was trying to get different ranks and different specialties. We didn't yet have designators then. Admiral Russell, I remember, was JAG.‡ He swore us in.

Well, I did get the rotation plans. And anytime I got a great deal of opposition, I would just say, "Well, why don't you put down why you're opposed to it?" That just ended it. They initialed it.

Paul Stillwell: They didn't want to admit it.

Captain Collins: No, they didn't want the chief to see their objections, and I knew that. But I took an awful lot of beating about it. And the most ridiculous thing was the question of why women should have to be rotated. And I said, "Well, how will they get

---
* Vice Admiral Thomas L. Sprague, USN, served as Chief of Naval Personnel from 22 February 1947 to 7 September 1949.
† The other six were Lieutenant Ann King, USN; Lieutenant Frances Willoughby, USN; Lieutenant Ellen Ford, USN; Lieutenant Doris Cranmore, USN; Lieutenant (junior grade) Doris Defenderfer, USN; and Lieutenant (junior grade) Betty Tennant, USN. Admiral Russell gave them the oaths on 15 October 1948.
‡ Rear Admiral George L. Russell, USN, served as the Navy's Judge Advocate General from 1948 to 1952.

to know the Navy? How will get to be promoted?" The men raising the objections didn't want them promoted. That was simple: "Don't rotate them. Don't promote them. Don't have them."

Paul Stillwell: Did you have a phased plan for bringing in further increments to get up to the 500 level?

Captain Collins: That came later, yes. I'll have to refresh my memory on that, because we had augmentation.[*] And when we started recruiting, I'll have to check. Lets see, I'm trying to think of the dates now. We became regular Navy in '48, and I stayed in that job, I guess, until '49 or '50. Then I was sent over to Secretary of Defense staff, which was a terrible job. I didn't have anything to do. Just horrible.

Paul Stillwell: What sort of things did you do during the time you were still at BuPers?

Captain Collins: Well, the big problem was to get all the women out of communications who'd been there for years and move them into other kinds of jobs. That was opposed by the commands that had these women, because they didn't want to lose them then. They were very skilled. And then trying to find new kinds of places for them was difficult because some commands didn't want them at all. Some wanted a great many. But they were still pretty limited kinds of assignments, and I'm speaking of the officers now. The enlisted, of course, had their ratings, so that was identifiable information at least.

Paul Stillwell: Was it a matter of negotiating with these commands on what kind of jobs they could be put into?

Captain Collins: Oh, definitely, yes.

Paul Stillwell: Are there any striking examples that stick out in your mind?

---

[*] Augmentation is the process by which a Naval Reserve officer is approved for a commission in the regular Navy.

Captain Collins: I know there were a lot, but I can't think of them at the moment. But a lot of the shore establishments were accustomed to women. The problem was then they didn't want to lose those they had, and then where would they put those coming in? I mean, it was a whole new idea to have women in a similar situation as men and rotated and promoted.

Paul Stillwell: Was there a question of whether the regular Navy women could be married or not?

Captain Collins: No, that had long since been solved. They could be married. That was dealt with in the early days. I think we solved that by early '43.[*] They could be married. And then the problem was that if they married Navy men, they'd be separated from each other anyhow. But there was no question about being married, enlisted and officer both.

Paul Stillwell: But pregnancy still meant automatic discharge.

Captain Collins: Yes, that's right.

Paul Stillwell: I don't think that was changed until about the 1970s.

Captain Collins: No, it wasn't. After I left the job, definitely.[†] It took a fight to allow them to stay in after having a child. And that was a big cultural change.

Paul Stillwell: Indeed.

Captain Collins: Yes. But I stayed, I think, about a year at SecDef, but I was most unhappy, because I didn't really have enough work to do, and I love to work.[‡] And I'd

---

[*] The first marriage by a WAVES officer was in April 1943 at Smith College. The bride was Ensign Shirley Bailey, USNR, and her husband was Ensign Fred Maiwurm, USNR.
[†] Captain Collins was Director of the WAVES from 1957 to 1962.
[‡] SecDef – Secretary of Defense.

had such interesting jobs up until that point in my career that I was most unhappy. Fortunately, I was selected to go to Stanford for a year's graduate work.*

Paul Stillwell: How did you spend that year in the SecDef job?

Captain Collins: I used to discipline myself. I found they had a fantastic library down there, and because of my interest in finance, I'd go down there for one hour in the morning and one hour in the afternoon. I wouldn't stay any longer than that, and I felt guilty doing that, but I just didn't have anything to do when I came back. You know, it was miserable.

Paul Stillwell: Was there any official assignment?

Captain Collins: Yes, I was in the big personnel office, but I'd been used to really thinking ahead and working things out. And what I had there was very routine. It'd take me about ten minutes probably to do any work I had. And that isn't what I'd been doing for years. So I was happy I was selected for Stanford.

Paul Stillwell: Why were you sent to that job? Were you the token woman in this office?

Captain Collins: I think I was part of the token Navy. The Navy was very opposed to the SecDef situation. The Air Force was right there, I tell you. But the Navy just was opposed, period. And so I think I was, in a sense, a token Navy number to go there.

Paul Stillwell: Well, it sounds like, "If we have to send somebody, well send somebody that we can't use somewhere else."

Captain Collins: Yes, that's right. I think that was it. Yes. Very definitely. I did know

---

* Stanford University, Palo Alto, California.

Steve Early, who then was deputy.*

Paul Stillwell: He had been Roosevelt's press secretary.†

Captain Collins: Yes. And I knew him very well, personally, socially. He may have been the one who put in a word. I don't know. I never knew that.

Captain Varian was then head of officer personnel, and he was very opposed to my going, because I was quite knowledgeable in terms of the women program, obviously.‡ He didn't want me to go, but if SecDef requested a person, they got that person. Now, I don't know that I was requested per se. I know I ended up in a miserable situation, from my point of view. I felt I wasn't really earning my pay, and I was very, very unhappy, thinking of how I could get out of there. And, fortunately, Stanford came along, so I was only there—oh, maybe not a whole year, I don't believe.

Paul Stillwell: When did you go to Stanford?

Captain Collins: I went in 1951, after the Korean War started.§ My relief over in BuPers was mighty busy. There was a buildup, recalling reserves. And I was sorry I wasn't there.

Paul Stillwell: But that didn't have an effect in the SecDef job?

Captain Collins: No. So I went to Stanford in '51, and I graduated in '52. There were 15 officers: submarine officers, aviators, line, black-shoe, and two other women officers. And it was a terrific year, really, because we could take graduate work across the board.

Paul Stillwell: And this was financed by the Navy.

---

* Steven T. Early served as Under Secretary of Defense, later retitled Deputy Secretary of Defense, 2 May 1949 to 30 September 1950.
† Early was White House press secretary from 1933 to 1945.
‡ Captain Donald C. Varian, USN.
§ The Korean War began on 25 June 1950, when six North Korean infantry division and three border constabulary brigades invaded South Korea.

Captain Collins: Yes. We got our full salary, and the Navy paid for everything.

We had a very interesting group. We all agreed, always at the beginning of each quarter, that we weren't going to knock ourselves out for A's, because the Navy really didn't care much. That's the silliest thing that ever happened. Not a one of us was going to be down here and somebody up here. So we all worked terrifically, and we'd take courses in which we didn't have undergraduate background. Since Stanford is very highly selective in terms of the students, we really had a tremendous job getting our A's in some of the courses.

Paul Stillwell: Did you have a chance to pick which courses you would take?

Captain Collins: Yes. The dean of education was really our mentor in terms of that, because he had been back in BuPers as either Director of Training, or Assistant Director during the war. So he was very knowledgeable about BuPers and the Navy organization.

I remember that I got into advanced statistics, which was way over my head, and I went to him and said, "I've made a mistake because I don't have the mathematical background to handle this. And no way do I want to fail a course." That was no problem to him; I just switched to something else. I'd had a course, and all the academy men had, so this was duck soup to them, of course. But that professor might as well have been speaking Chinese, as far as I was concerned. Fortunately, I never needed it again. That was the only problem I had. We all really had a wonderful time together. Our studying was so intense we wouldn't even have a glass of wine because it affected our retention, absolutely no question about it.

Paul Stillwell: Were you aiming toward a specific major?

Captain Collins: Well, we all got master's degrees in education, but most of us took other things as well: business administration, public administration, political science. The head of the political science department wanted me to write a thesis and stay on and get a doctorate in that subject. But I said, "I don't think I'd really have any use for a doctorate in the Navy." And I don't think I would've. It would have been nice to have, but it would have taken a tremendous effort while holding a regular job.

Paul Stillwell: Did you write a thesis as part of the master's degree?

Captain Collins: No, we didn't. Some of our courses had 15 textbooks, and that took care of it. It was the most strenuous year academically I've ever been through but very, very worthwhile. I particularly valued the opportunity to take political science and public administration, you know, the management side of that, which was very helpful in what we were all going into.

In '52, after a year of this course, I was assigned as assistant director of naval personnel, Com 12.[*] It was unbelievable what that caused in the commandant's office. The attitude was that a woman couldn't do the job.

Paul Stillwell: Who was the commandant?

Captain Collins: I think it was Rodgers.[†]

The personnel director on the staff was a commander, and he was a mustang.[‡] Any time he would have to write a dispatch or a letter to BuPers, he'd just crack up. So I just said, "Why don't you let me do it?" So he got to like me very much. I was very useful to him, and we became very good friends. And if there had to be a telephone call to BuPers, I said, "Let me do it, because I know the old grapevine back there very well."

So then he came up for retirement, and my orders came. I was to take over as the director, but Admiral Rodgers said, "I will not have a woman as director of naval personnel."[§]

Paul Stillwell: This would be both men and women, obviously, you were directing.

---

[*] Com 12 – Commandant of the 12th Naval District, with headquarters on Treasure Island, San Francisco.
[†] Rear Admiral Bertram J. Rodgers, USN, served as Com 12 from 1950 to 1954.
[‡] "Mustang" is Navy slang for a former enlisted man or woman who has risen through the ranks to become an officer. In this case the mustang, her boss, was Commander James W. Hager, USN.
[§] Hager retired from active duty on 1 June 1953.

Captain Collins: Oh, it was a staff of 300, which was administering 50,000 reserve and regular personnel over three states, Nevada, part of Arizona, and the northern part of California. I had enlisted men and officers, male officers. Big staff of civilians. Also, the job was big, because San Francisco was the entry port for everything going and coming to the Pacific.

Paul Stillwell: You probably relished a job like that.

Captain Collins: I did, I loved it. But, he said, "I will not have a woman." The head of shore establishment assignments in BuPers—I didn't know him at that time—was a Commander Caspari.* He went to Admiral Sprague, and he said, "She has the finest personnel record I think we have in the Navy."†

Because I'd had a tremendous amount of experience, and I'd had the Harvard business and Stanford, and that's what I enjoyed doing. And I never received anything less than a 4.0 in any job I was in, even that horrible one in SecDef. They just gave it for my doing practically nothing.

So Caspari took it to Admiral Sprague, and he said, "I've prepared a dispatch here, Admiral." This message said that unless Com 12 would take me, that he would leave the billet vacant. So, under those agreeable circumstances, I was accepted.

Paul Stillwell: Did you feel a sense of awkwardness under those circumstances?

Captain Collins: I didn't have the welcome mat; that's for sure. Fortunately, Admiral Rodgers was relieved, and the whole thing changed with the new commander, Admiral Redman.‡ A reporter from *The Christian Science Monitor* came, because it was very unusual to have women as personnel directors even in civilian companies, and I was it as

---

* Lieutenant Commander William J. Caspari, USN.
† Vice Admiral Thomas L. Sprague, USN, had been Chief of Naval Personnel from 1947 to 1949 so Captain Collins was evidently remembering him from that earlier period. In 1953 Vice Admiral Laurence T. Dubose, USN, was Chief of Naval Personnel until 2 February, when he was relieved by Vice Admiral James L. Holloway Jr., USN.
‡ Rear Admiral John R. Redman, served as Com 12 from 1954 to 1957.

far as the Navy was concerned. My having the job was a big thing in those days, so this woman reporter wanted to write a story about it. I said, "Well, that's fine with me."

She said, "How do the enlisted men and male officers like working for you?"

I said, "I have no idea. I like them, and we work together. You can go and tell them that they don't have to worry about their fitness reports. They can tell you whatever they want to." The article came out all right, and I was pleased, because I think *The Christian Science Monitor* is a very prestigious newspaper.[*]

Paul Stillwell: Were you promoted to commander in that job?

Captain Collins: Yes. Kay Dougherty and I were the first women commanders selected by selection board, which was pretty exciting.[†]

Paul Stillwell: Were there separate selection boards for women?

Captain Collins: Yes, at that time there were. The boards had men on them, of course. I don't even think we had a woman on it then. Later, during my regime as director of the WAVES, I insisted on women being on the boards too.

Paul Stillwell: Please tell me more about what you did in that job once you had it.

Captain Collins: Well, this was the first real impact of a career woman encountering chauvinistic attitudes from a senior flag man, and it was Rodgers. Fortunately for me, he had to accept me or have no one. Builds your morale tremendously. But he asked me what my job was. I outlined the geographical area we covered, and it amounted to 50,000 total reserve and active duty. I think my staff was 300, made up of civilians, male officers, and enlisted males, and then enlisted women, and women officers too. I was nervous about it, because I didn't know how the male part of the Navy would look at me

---

[*] Captain Collins's memoir indicates that the interview with *Christian Science Monitor* was in December 1953.
[†] Kathryn Dougherty and Winifred Quick were promoted to commander with the same date of rank, 1 July 1953. Dougherty retired as a commander in 1965.

as their boss. In addition to making out their fitness reports, I made out fitness reports for all of those assigned to all of the reserve units. That amounted to a tremendous number. They had a big reserve organization, which was separate from me but on the same staff, so we coordinated.

Our people assigned all the enlisted and officers coming into that area for shore assignments. We also handled all the disciplinary cases, male, coming from the Pacific.

Paul Stillwell: They were just dumped there?

Captain Collins: Dumped there, and we had to deal with them. I worked with legal all the time. But they were extra numbers that we had to handle. It was a vibrant job, definitely, and I loved it.

Paul Stillwell: Did you also get into disbursing and travel pay and that sort of thing?

Captain Collins: Well, not personally; that, of course, that was handled by another department. But when officers and enlisted men came in, we'd have to endorse their orders, and then they would go to disbursing. I had a male officer in charge of officer personnel and another one in charge of enlisted personnel. Both of them were wonderful.

I had only one discipline problem the whole time I was there. That was with my officer who kept coming in late. This was new to me, and I didn't know just how to handle it. I called him in one morning, and I said, "Rowan, I must tell you, I'm very disappointed in you. I've given you an excellent fitness report, because you well deserve it. However, you are causing a morale problem among your civilians and among your military because you're late every day. If I can get here, why can't you?"

He said, "I'll never let you down again."

That sounds simple. But in those days, the relationship was different when the boss was a woman. Now it's easier. But that was the only time I ever had a discipline problem.

Paul Stillwell: But you felt awkward initially?

Captain Collins: I did, of course. You would. But I wanted to handle it right, because he was very competent, and he'd done beautifully. I said, "Unless you change—I'm just talking to you—I can't ever give you the kind of fitness report I did in the past because of what you're doing to your personnel."

That was enough. That was all he needed to hear. But it was also an experience for me in knowing just how to handle it, because I had no guideline. No woman had ever been in that kind of job before, and frankly I just wanted to handle it well. It seems ridiculous in retrospect now, but that's what it was.

Paul Stillwell: Were the enlisted people in Com 12 detailed from your office, or was that done from Washington?

Captain Collins: Oh, all enlisted were sent to Com 12, and the man on my staff who was in charge of enlisted personnel detailed them. He inspected the barracks there on Treasure Island, and he did all the additional jobs that go with that kind of thing.* Com 12 was a vibrant, moving place. It was the biggest West Coast area of personnel and all.

Admiral Rodgers, fortunately, left early and Admiral Redman came. He and I got along beautifully, very close. I'd go to all the staff meetings, which I didn't before. I worked for the assistant chief of staff for personnel, a captain. Unfortunately, some of them are totally unknowledgeable about how to treat people. I remember one time Captain Heald called me when I was getting my hair done at noon.† He said I had to come immediately. I was so angry, because I was running the whole thing. He was just sitting there. So I came in as fast as I could, and he said, "I'd like you to call Washington."

I said, "All right." I went to the phone. I said, "Too late. I can't get anyone." For five days, I couldn't get anyone. He never did that again. I was so angry at him for trying to dominate me like that. And he got the message.

---

* Treasure Island is a man-made island in San Francisco Bay, located between San Francisco and Oakland. It served as the site of a world's fair in 1939-40, then was converted for use as a Navy base during and after World War II.
† Captain Wilton S. Heald, USN.

Paul Stillwell: So he was essentially treating you as a secretary.

Captain Collins: He was and also very arrogantly. Because I did all the work, and the reason he didn't want to call Washington was that he was scared. Oh, he wouldn't touch the phone. I said, "Why don't you try? I haven't been able to get them."

Paul Stillwell: So once you made your point, then you could get through, of course.

Captain Collins: After five days, I was able to get through, because I knew everybody back there. It was very simple.

Captain McGirr was another one, and he knew absolutely nothing about personnel.* He'd just come over and interrogate me. One day he came over and put his feet on my desk. I was so angry. I thought to myself, "Should I continue in the Navy, or shall I knock his feet off?"

But then he wanted to become a lawyer. And that was the period in which no one could get released from the Navy, probably because the Korean War was in progress. But I used to go back to BuPers frequently, because the people at the top in Com 12 wanted me to go back. The commandant wanted me to go back, chief of staff, and especially my assistant chief of staff for personnel. I'd have a lot of fun, because I knew everybody back there and I'd take care of their business. Captain McGirr just bugged everybody, particularly me. I said, "Well, why don't you write up a letter that you want to get out for this reason, to go to law school, and I'll take it back and see."

I went in to captain detail. It happened to be one of the officers that I went around the country with on that classification project, and he became a really close friend. And he said, "Winnie, what's your problem?"

I said, "Do you know the name of Captain McGirr?"

"Oh, that's right, you've got that fool, haven't you?"

I said, "Well, I have a letter here, because he wants to get out of the Navy to go to law school. Now, regulations say no one can be released."

---

* Captain William P. McGirr, USN.

He said, "We have exceptions all the time." You know, he got those orders before I could get back. It was the first time Captain McGirr ever thought I was worth anything.

I said, "Well, he made an exception because of your record." I didn't say what the exception was. Anyway, he got out, and, I tell you, there was cheering on my staff that day.[*]

But it was, to me, a really fun job. I loved it. And I had tremendous staff. I liked them, and they knew I liked them. We accomplished big jobs very nicely.

Paul Stillwell: Well, in a way, its nice to have a boss that doesn't know what's going on because then you can run it.

Captain Collins: Well, yes, and he didn't know how to run it, let's face it. But he would treat me really very arrogantly and dominate me. The chief of staff would call me directly, because they thought my immediate boss was so horrible. So I knew the admiral would change it if the assistant chief of staff wrote me a bad fitness card. I don't know if he did or not, but I got magnificent fitness reports.

Later on, when I was being selected for Assistant Chief of Naval Personnel and director of the WAVES, I didn't know any of those on my selection board. One of the board members came to me later, after seeing my fitness reports, and said, "We thought maybe Admiral Redman was in love with you."

I said, "No. He's a remarkable man."

While I was there at Com 12, an AlNav came out that all commanders must have a sword.[†] It didn't say that women should have swords too. But I kind of laughed about it. Obviously, I was the only woman commander on the staff there, since Kay Dougherty was the only other one in the United States Navy. Some of my staff said, "We want to have a little happy hour over at the club after work on Friday. Can you come?"

I said, "Sure."

---

[*] Captain McGirr, who was in the Naval Academy class of 1925, retired on 1 January 1954.
[†] AlNav – a message addressed to the entire Navy.

So I went into this room, and suddenly the chief of staff appeared. I thought, "That's odd. They didn't tell me he was coming." In a few minutes, Admiral Redman came in, and I said, "They didn't tell me this was going to be this kind of a party."

He said, "Well, we have a special occasion. I've been worrying the fact that you didn't have a sword."

So in came two of my staff, carrying sofa pillows, and on them was the case to hold a sword. This case was made with sequins on one side and my name on the other. They presented it to me, and I practically fell backwards because inside was a paring knife.[*]

Paul Stillwell: Didn't you have to wear a regular Navy sword?

Captain Collins: No, no. It didn't say all in the AlNav. It just said all commanders and above had to have them, see. And that's why this wonderful commandant gave this to me. It was his idea completely to have this made for me and give it to me. So you can see that times changed for me in terms of my time in the Navy in Com 12. I enjoyed it very much. He also gave me a lovely party when I was selected for commander.

Then I was selected to go to the CinCNELM staff.[†] That was a real trauma for the senior officers on the staff in London, because I was the first senior woman officer to be assigned there. After I got there, I read a letter that had come to CinCNELM from the Chief of Naval Personnel, Admiral Holloway.[‡] He said, "She is very _attractive_." Underlined, see? It didn't have a word about anything I'd ever done. I was so infuriated, and I said, "When will we ever end this kind of thing and say something about qualifications." Not one word was included in that letter. This was what women faced constantly, both in and out of the Navy.

In other words, BuPers was trying to sell me in terms of being a woman—that I wouldn't be a horse face, I guess. I'd be attractive. But there was nothing whatsoever about qualification, and I'd had a fairly interesting career up to that point. They could've

---

[*] A photo of Admiral Redman making the presentation is on page 115 of Captain Collins's book.
[†] CinCNELM – Commander in Chief U.S. Naval Forces Eastern Atlantic and Mediterranean.
[‡] Vice Admiral James L. Holloway, Jr., USN, served as Chief of the Bureau of Naval Personnel from 1953 to 1958. His oral history is in the Columbia University collection.

said something, I figured. But, no, that was the selling point, see. I was secretly very infuriated, but that's what constantly went on. There's no question about it.

Paul Stillwell: Did you find that you had to deliberately stifle yourself on many occasions?

Captain Collins: Definitely, definitely. And before I was selected to go over there, I went to five different desks, including the commander desk. Admiral Mack was the commander detailer then.* Well, it was a selling job. He was scared to death about having a woman go over there. You know: "The sky's going to fall, the British will collapse"—the whole thing. And I had to go to the CinCNELM desk and something else. At that point we invented "The Fig Leaf Society." See, if you weren't a woman, there'd be no problem. And that's what it really was. The fact that a woman would be assigned over there just horrified them. What would they do with a woman? And that prevailed for many, many years. Now I think it has, of course, greatly dissipated. But still, when I talk to some of the younger officers, the chauvinistic attitudes are still there.

For example, when women first went to the Naval Academy, there was a tremendous trauma there.†

Paul Stillwell: The Naval Institute has interviewed some of those first ones.‡

Captain Collins: Dean Davidson was one of my close friends, and he said he thought it was the greatest thing that ever happened to the young men, because they came there thinking they were the cream of the crop.§ Then the women were highly intelligent, highly selected, and would outdistance them in the courses. Admiral Lawrence's

---

* Commander William P. Mack, USN. The oral history of Mack, who retired as a vice admiral, is in the Naval Institute collection.
† Women were first admitted to the Naval Academy as midshipmen in the summer of 1976, the same year the other federal service academies admitted women cadets.
‡ Susan Sweeney of the Naval Institute staff was the interviewer.
§ Dr. Bruce K. Davidson was the Naval Academy's academic dean from 1 July 1971 to 20 July 1985.

daughter got the top engineering award.* My husband was going to give her a wristwatch in recognition of her achievement. But the people at the Naval Academy had picked out a man's watch. I said to him, "Call them, because I bet they have a man's watch." Sure enough.

The person he talked to said, "It's all engraved, Admiral."

Howard said, "I don't care. I'm paying, and she's going to have a woman's watch. You can engrave a woman's watch. My wife has a diamond one from the Navy League, fully engraved on the back."

They just couldn't think of this award in terms of a woman. It had to be always in the male category.

Then the women beat the men in pistol shooting and that kind of thing. It's shattering.

Paul Stillwell: A real blow to the ego.

Captain Collins: Oh, terrible. But the more recent women midshipmen tell me it's easier now. I talk to them every once in a while, some of those girls I meet. But that first class had a very rough time. I know it.

Paul Stillwell: There was a striking thing, though, that as subsequent classes of women came in, the first class didn't especially try to help them. They sort of said, "Well, we had to go through it, and they should too."

Captain Collins: Oh, did they? Now, that's crazy, isn't it? I would think they would've helped them.

Paul Stillwell: I would've thought so too.

---

* Midshipman Wendy B. Lawrence, USN, stood 12th of the 966 graduates in the Naval Academy class of 1981. Vice Admiral William P. Lawrence, USN, served as superintendent of the academy from August 1978 to August 1981.

Captain Collins: That's surprising to me. Because that's never been my attitude. I always try and help women. But maybe they felt they had it so tough, "See if you can take it." That kind of attitude, perhaps, and resentful, in a sense, that they had it so tough, I'm sure.

Paul Stillwell: Oh, surely.

Captain Collins: And they did, there's no question about it. Because, not only did the young males resent them, but then they resented them more when they were achievers in many areas which weren't part of a woman's prerogative, in a sense, there. So I admire what they went through.

Paul Stillwell: Another situation they had was that the parents of boys who weren't selected for the academy were very resentful of these women who perhaps deprived them of an opportunity.

Captain Collins: Oh, I hadn't even thought of that. But, of course, they would be. Did the superintendent get some letters on that kind of thing?

Paul Stillwell: I don't know. He might well have.

Captain Collins: But how did you know about it then?

Paul Stillwell: My assistant has interviewed a number of the first women midshipmen for our oral history program, and they told her about this.

Captain Collins: Well, that would be very true.

I told you the enlisted men were so resentful about having women in the Navy. I think they were frightened of them in terms of their educational achievements. That it would take something from them and they didn't want that kind of competition. So it's better. It's not solved yet. Probably never will be, but it's much better certainly. I've worked with a tremendous number of wonderful Navy men, and I also worked with a lot who were very opposed in every possible way. And I was a focal point in each of those, yes. So you learn diplomacy fast.

Paul Stillwell: I'm struck by the parallels between the situations you're describing for women and the ones that black men faced.

Captain Collins: Oh, almost identical, yes. Very much so. Right down the line, a black man could not be an officer. And if he were an officer, whom would he associate with? I mean, the social structure. And the same was true with women. If a woman was a naval officer, what would we do about social occasions? It was nervousness on the part of the males, really.

Paul Stillwell: Well, you talked about the situation of going on liberty with these two petty officers. Admiral Gravely, as an ensign, went on liberty with black enlisted men from his ship because the white officers wouldn't.* So he got arrested by the military police for impersonating an officer, first, and then fraternizing with enlisted men.

Captain Collins: I can believe it. I met him in Washington here, and I can't think what occasion it was. But we did talk about that very subject, because I'm sure it was close to him, as it is close to me.

Paul Stillwell: And he said that blacks were often routed into communications, as women were.

Captain Collins: That's right. Nobody wanted to be a communicator, so that's where we went.

Paul Stillwell: Please tell me what happened once you reported to the CinCNELM staff.

---

* Vice Admiral Samuel L. Gravely, USN (Ret.), was the first black officer to be selected for flag rank in the U.S. Navy. His oral history in the Naval Institute's collection. See also Samuel L. Gravely with Paul Stillwell, *Trailblazer: the U.S. Navy's First Black Admiral* (Annapolis: Naval Institute Press, 2010).

Captain Collins: The man I was to relieve on the staff was a commander. He was in Garmisch with his wife for some leave, and he took a wrong step at dusk and fell 5,000 feet.[*] It was very tragic. He and I had exchanged letters about the job before he died, and he sounded like a delightful man. In one of them he said, "I'm getting a lot of teasing about having a woman relieve me in this job," and so forth. But it was really a tragic incident. I became very good friends with the wife, and I've seen her many times since then.

Paul Stillwell: I'm curious how that assignment came about. You were pioneering in roles for a regular Navy woman. There was no career pattern established.

Captain Collins: No, no. That came later. At the time you were just assigned.

Paul Stillwell: Could you signify a preference for duty?

Captain Collins: Well, let me tell you the situation. Nine doctors in Oak Knoll told me I had cancer.[†] It turned out I didn't, but I went through a very difficult turmoil. My good friend, Commander Caspari of shore establishments, said, "You've really worked yourself to death out there. Why don't I get you a nice assignment somewhere?" He debated about Italy, and then he thought London was very quiet, because CinCNELM had a wonderful staff there. So he said, "Why don't I send you there?" It was kind of a compassionate, I guess, assignment in a sense, although it turned out a little differently.

When I arrived, I was assigned to work for the assistant chief of staff for administration. About the third day I was in CinCNELM, my new boss said, "I want you to go to Paris for a meeting."

I said, "Yes, sir. What should I do? What's the name of the committee?"

He said, "I don't want you to make any commitment about CinCNELM."

I said, "Well, you're pretty sure of that. I don't even know what it's about."

---

[*] Garmisch-Partenkirchen is a mountain resort town in Bavaria, Germany.
[†] Naval Hospital Oakland was commissioned 1 July 1942 on the site of the former Oak Knoll Golf and Country Club, on the hills on the east side of San Francisco Bay.

I went through the files and tried to find information. This meeting concerned the armed forces agreements involving the individual U.S. services—the Air Force, the Army, and so forth—in the NATO countries.* But I didn't know that until I got there. So I was really horrified to be representing CinCNELM and not knowing anything about the subject. But I went there, and I went into where it was being held. There were two generals there, one Air Force and one Army. I said to them, "Gentlemen, I must tell you that I absolutely know nothing about this. The man I was to relieve was a commander, and he was killed at Garmisch."

That emotional appeal got me over. Because they said, "You just sit between us, my dear, and don't you worry." But I was embarrassed for the Navy to think that they'd put me in the position of not even knowing what the meeting was about. In three months I was chairman of that group. I had all the representatives from all over Europe there. By then I was well informed, and I had the lawyer right beside me. That's the way you should do it. Because it really was a legal organization, although they had some lawyers in it, representing. But it was a terrible situation for me to go to the meeting totally unknowledgeable and then have the two other services have general officers there.

Paul Stillwell: Why do you think CinCNELM did that?

Captain Collins: Because the boss was a captain and an alcoholic. He didn't know what was going on. Or maybe he wanted to embarrass me. I don't know. Could be some of both.

Paul Stillwell: Yes, but you don't deliberately embarrass your command in order to embarrass an individual.

Captain Collins: You wouldn't think so. I'm sure he didn't know what it was. I didn't recognize that he was intoxicated, but I went off to talk to one of the chiefs, and I said, "He says I should come back the same day. That's quite a trip to do."

---

* NATO – North Atlantic Treaty Organization, which was established in 1949 as a means of coordinating defense against a potential attack from the Soviet Union.

He said, "Nah, just forget that."

He didn't say, "He's an alcoholic." He didn't say anything derogatory, but he gave me the general impression, "You do whatever you think you should, because he won't remember." That was kind of what he was saying, and I thought he did it very diplomatically.

But I didn't come back that day, obviously. I really got some very good information from these two generals. And, of course, I didn't know I was going to be chairman in three months, but, boy, once I knew that, I went to work on it.

Paul Stillwell: I wonder if it was also symptomatic of the Navy not really desiring to cooperate that much with the other services.

Captain Collins: I don't think that was it. I really can't believe that. Because it was to their advantage to cooperate.

Paul Stillwell: I see.

Captain Collins: Because we'd all three go to a country to try and get more privileges for our armed forces, or recreation, or any of the things. You see, the United States signed an agreement with the other countries in NATO about U.S. military personnel being there.

Paul Stillwell: It sounds like a status-of-forces agreement.

Captain Collins: Yes, and it included the regulations that they must follow. In some cases we had to request changes to the agreement, because it just didn't make sense from our standpoint or our personnel. It was to the advantage of our people—so I don't think that this captain wanted to avoid cooperating with the others.

Paul Stillwell: Well, maybe the generals were there because the Army and Air Force would have more people in Europe than the Navy.

Captain Collins: That's right. I think that's part of it, very definitely. I don't think Admiral Cassady knew that this agreement existed, because I'm absolutely sure the captain hadn't kept him informed.* Because they should have had somebody of higher rank than a commander there to represent the Navy. Obviously this commander had represented CinCNELM before he died, although I couldn't find a single thing in his files about it. So I don't know what kind of representation was there. But I enjoyed it after I became a little knowledgeable, and I'd meet them in different countries, which I liked.

Later Admiral Boone became commander in chief there.† We were on a full alert all the time. The Egyptian Crisis started, and so it was a hectic time, militarily. The British very much disliked us because of our stand we took over the Suez intervention.‡ We would not go with them on that, and so the British were taking it out on the U.S. servicemen who were nearby. We took all of our enlisted people out of uniform, because they were getting beaten up at that time in Great Britain. But it was an exciting time in terms of being on the alert all the time.

Paul Stillwell: Do you remember any specific instances in regard to these conditions that you were negotiating with the NATO countries?

Captain Collins: No, no, I don't, really. I don't think I kept that many notes on it.

Paul Stillwell: Was this the bulk of your work?

Captain Collins: No. Let's see. I had about five jobs. I was the CinCNELM representative for all the officer and enlisted messes throughout Europe, which involved a tremendous amount of money. And they got in a very bad situation about a recreational

---

* Admiral John H. Cassady, USN, served as Commander in Chief U.S. Naval Forces Eastern Atlantic and Mediterranean (CinCNELM) from March 1954 to May 1956.
† Admiral Walter F. Boone, USN, served as Commander in Chief U.S. Naval Forces Eastern Atlantic and Mediterranean (CinCNELM) from May 1956 to February 1958.
‡ On 26 July 1956 President Gamal Nasser of Egypt announced that his country was nationalizing the Suez Canal Company. Israeli forces invaded Egypt's Sinai Peninsula on 29 October 1956. Britain and France then intervened militarily on behalf of Israel in an unsuccessful attempt to secure the Suez Canal, which was damaged and closed to traffic. Rather than support the British and French, the United States asked for a United Nations resolution to end the fighting. A cease-fire took effect on 6 November.

hotel they had in Italy. I used to go to see the Supply Corps people and have them go over the papers because I didn't feel it was adequate. But I had to keep a sharp check on that. I was a vulnerable court-martial case in any instance of wrongdoing.

Then I was also the representative for our VIP protocol office. When Admiral Boone arrived, he said he wanted the staff officers to go. My immediate boss was then Captain Kelly, who had been an aide to Secretary Matthews, I believe.* And what I had to do was to call up people. It was a very busy protocol office, as you can well imagine, but we had no watch list for meeting VIPs. I remember I called one captain, and I said, "Captain, you're on the list to meet So-and-so."

He said, "I'll be goddamned if I'll have a commander telling me what to do."

I said, "You know what, Captain, I'll be goddamned if I'll have you talking to me that way." I hung up the phone.

So I went in to Captain Kelly, and I said, "I'm getting sick of this. Why can't we have a watch list?"

And, "Blah-blah-blah. Let's go to the chief of staff and ask."

He was an aide who expected to be an admiral instantly, though he never made it. He said, "I'm not going to risk that."

I said, "What are we risking? I think it's wrong for me to have to call captains and tell them that they have the duty. This one made it very clear, and I agree with him, but I'm not going to have somebody talking to me that way." Then I said, "Then if you won't go with me, can I go to the chief of staff?"

He said, "Sure, if you want to put your neck out like that."

I thought, "Neck out? I thought it was just Navy policy to have it laid out and have the chief of staff sign it, so I wouldn't be doing it on my own. With a watch list it would be simple to call them up." I went to the chief of staff, and he agreed with me completely.

Paul Stillwell: Who was he?

---

* Francis P. Matthews served as Secretary of the Navy from 25 May 1949 to 30 July 1951.

Captain Collins: Rear Admiral Walter Price.*

I had one other job. I know I had four jobs, and the good part about them was that I could work my schedule and be away from CinCNELM most of the time.

Paul Stillwell: Why did you want to be away most of the time?

Captain Collins: Oh, it was a terrible staff, really.

One time the admiral wrote a letter to all the captains and said, "There's not a single one on the staff who can write a letter." And this was a prestigious staff of carefully selected people. That was when I was put in charge of getting a professor from American University to teach the senior officers how to write a letter. Enviable job. Absolutely. Fortunately, we had a lot of fun with it, so nobody was mad at me about it. But it was a situation in which everyone was pretty much disgruntled and unhappy.

We could take leave from CinCNELM if we would give our telephone number every night where we were in Europe. That was impossible almost, and terribly expensive, but otherwise, you couldn't take leave. That's it. The previous admiral used to take the staff when he'd make visits on his plane. Nobody went. So I would say morale wasn't of the highest. When I got my orders, all the captains said, "Winnie, we want to take you out to lunch and buy you a drink." Then they said, "Actually, we have a very subtle reason for taking you. We want to raffle your orders off to all the captains on the staff. We're so envious."

I said, "How much? What's the starting bid?"

They said, "$100.00."

After they went through this, I said, "I hate to discourage you, but there's one obstacle."

They said, "What's that?"

I said, "You'll never pass the physical."†

But I had a lot of good friends there, and that was a redeeming factor of the whole thing. But I was there only 13 months.

---

* Rear Admiral Walter H. Price, USN.
† This was said tongue in cheek, because her next assignment was to serve as director of the WAVES.

Paul Stillwell: Did you have many dealings with the British during that period?

Captain Collins: Oh, yes. I had visited the WRNS headquarters, and the mayor of London had me to lunch because I was the first senior woman American officer there.* As for the Wrens, all of the British family women were Navy commissioned. So I met many of them at very lovely parties. When I left, Admiral Boone of CinCNELM did not give me a party, but the British Wrens gave me a party, and they had the whole cabinet there. Can you believe it? They're very prestigious women, but they do not have full status. They don't have the rank. They don't get the pay. They don't have any retirement, but they're magnificent top-drawer women from Great Britain. I got to know them very well and admired them tremendously. And so that was a very pleasant experience for me in that regard.

But most of the time we had such little time off that I didn't have much time for sightseeing or socializing, because I worked six days a week. Then I was on call during the night for messages, so it was pretty hectic and you can see why I was working out my rotation program to other kinds of jobs. I almost had it complete. I'd be away on four different committees, you see, and I thought, "Well, now it's going to be very good, very interesting." But I was in Paris at one of the committees, and I got a call from Admiral Boone's aide. The aide and I were very good friends, and so I was surprised when he was formal with me. I said, "What did I do, lose an information dispatch?" I thought, "I have done something pretty bad."

Then Admiral Boone came on the phone, and he said, "I have the honor of telling you that I have a confidential dispatch from Admiral Holloway that you've been selected as Assistant Chief of Naval Personnel." That's the last I ever saw of Admiral Boone.† He never had me come to his office or congratulate him, or nothing. I got back at him later, though. Anyhow, that's the way it was.

Paul Stillwell: How did you get back at him?

---

* WRNS – Women's Royal Naval Service. The women were nicknamed "Wrens" because of the acronym.
† Admiral Walter F. Boone, USN, retired from active duty in 1960 and died in 1995 at age 97.

Captain Collins: Well, when I got out of the Navy, I was in the Washington, D.C., Navy League. Then, in about a year, I became the first national vice president, the first woman ever as national vice president. And I was assigned membership drive. So I picked out all the senior admirals who weren't Navy League members, and I wrote letters, asking them to be life members. When Admiral Boone wrote back, he said he couldn't afford it. Four stars.

So I wrote to him again and said, "Dear Admiral Boone, I'm so very distressed about your financial situation. I would assist you, but I'm only a captain. You could help me, however, if you would tell me what we should tell the civilians in the United States about joining the Navy League if a four-star admiral won't. Sincerely."

He wrote back, "Here's my check. If you see the blots on the paper, its because you made me cry so much."

So he had a nice sense of humor about it at least. We're good friends now. He lives in Washington. But he was not admired as a leader.

Well, from the CinCNELM staff I went to Washington to be assistant chief, and we can cover that in our next meeting.

Paul Stillwell: I look forward to the next time.

aptain Collins: Oh, good.

Interview Number 2 with Captain Winifred Quick Collins, U.S. Navy (Retired)
Place: Captain Collins's apartment, Washington, D.C.
Date: Wednesday, 5 November 1986
Interviewer: Paul Stillwell

Captain Collins: I couldn't recall the names of the first women sworn in. Now, actually, there were eight, but they only took the photograph of this many of us. And they got the names down there. That's John Sullivan, Secretary of the Navy, and George Russell, JAG.[*]

Paul Stillwell: This was released in October 1948.

Captain Collins: Yes, we were the first women sworn into the regular Navy.

Paul Stillwell: I'll just read the names: Captain Joy B. Hancock, Lieutenant Commander Winifred R. Quick, Lieutenant (junior grade) Betty Rae Tennant—oh, those are the only ones in the picture. I see.

Captain Collins: So those, plus five others whose names I don't have.[†] Maybe somewhere I do, but that's the best I could come up with.

Paul Stillwell: The photo file number is 706215.

Captain Collins: Yes, that's right.

Paul Stillwell: All right. We had gotten to the point last week when you were nominated to be director of the WAVES, so could you resume the narrative at that point, please.

---

[*] John L. Sullivan served as Secretary of the Navy from 18 September 1947 to 24 May 1949. Rear Admiral George L. Russell, USN, served as the Navy's Judge Advocate General from 1948 to 1952.
[†] The other five were Ann King, Frances Willoughby, Ellen Ford, Doris Cranmore, and Doris Defenderfer. See Jean Ebbert and Marie-Beth Hall, *Crossed Currents: Navy Women from WWI to Tailhook* (Washington: Brassey's, 1993).

Captain Collins: Right. This was in London when I was informed. The Wrens gave me a very beautiful cocktail party in which they had most of the top officials in the British government attending. And the Wrens, as you probably know, are not part of the regular British Navy. They are really an auxiliary and are paid much less and have no retirement privileges. But they are composed of some of the women of outstanding families in Great Britain. So it was great pleasure that I got acquainted with them and got to know them very well.

Paul Stillwell: So were they somewhat comparable to the way the WACS were in the beginning in this country.

Captain Collins: Yes, similar, yes, strictly as an auxiliary. And they still exist that way.

Paul Stillwell: Well, that takes some dedication if you don't even get the privileges of the regular people.

Captain Collins: That's right. Well, of course, that's pretty much true of women, in general, in their work in Great Britain. The major exception is that they have a Prime Minister, but the women in most jobs get much less than men of comparable kind of occupation.* So it's in keeping with their tradition and treatment of women, in general.

My first call was on Admiral Burke, Chief of Naval Operations, whom I had never met, but, of course, I knew of his reputation very well.† And in my spick and span captain's uniform, I called on him. He got up from his desk and came to greet me and he said, "You have the prettiest blue eyes I've ever seen."

I said, "Admiral, now what do I say?" He completely threw my protocol. But he was a really delightful man. From then on, we became very close friends, and I'm a great admirer of him. I see him continuously. And I am going to make a call on him very shortly.

---

* Margaret Thatcher served as Prime Minister of the United Kingdom, 4 May 1979 to 28 November 1990.
† Admiral Arleigh A. Burke, USN, served as Chief of Naval Operations from 17 August 1955 to 1 August 1961. His oral history is in the Naval Institute collection.

The other person who was a tremendous help to me was Secretary Thomas Gates.* One of the first things he did after I called on him, he said, "Are you having any trouble with any of your programs?"

I said, "Mr. Secretary, I'm having trouble with every single program."

He said, "Well, I tell you what I'll do. I'll invite some of the key admirals to a luncheon, and we'll have a couple of cocktails. And then we sit down to lunch, I'm going to turn to you and say, 'Now, tell me are you having any problems?'" Which he did. And then he would say to this admiral, "Well, Jack, can't you do something about that?" And, "Tom, why can't you settle this?" So that was a tremendous support and backing.

Paul Stillwell: Can you at this point recount what some of those problems were that you enumerated?

Captain Collins: Yes, I certainly can. First of all, there was great—really, at some top level—Chief of Naval Personnel in Admiral Page Smith.† My feeling was he had total disinterest in women in the Navy and was not supportive of me and many of the things I wished to do. Recruiting, both officer and enlisted, was very bad. I didn't think we were getting the quality we should. And I'll explain later how I corrected that.

We had another very critical problem in that when a senior lieutenant commander or commander woman was nominated for a billet, often the commanding officer would accept the idea, and then he would say "No." So I went down to the head of performance and I said, "I don't understand what's going on." And what the ONI was doing was sending not a clearance, a secret clearance or whatever was required of the billet, but they were sending to the commanding officer a report such as, "This woman is living with another woman," or, "I've seen her embrace another woman."‡

They were misinterpreting the culture of women and comparing it with men. But they were leaving the responsibility strictly up the CO, instead of doing the job they

---

* Thomas S. Gates, Jr., served as Secretary of the Navy from 1 April 1957 to 7 June 1959.
† Vice Admiral Harold Page Smith, USN, served as Chief of Naval Personnel from 31 January 1958 to 12 February 1960. So he was not the bureau chief at the outset of Captain Quick's tenure as Assistant Chief of Naval Personnel for Women
‡ ONI – Office of Naval Intelligence.

should do. When I found this out, I was really infuriated. So I asked for a meeting with them. When I walked in, there were nine civilian men there, so I felt very confident if nine would come that they were considering it carefully. I said that I had a problem in that I understood they were not giving clearance, which I recalled was their responsibility as the intelligence branch of the Navy. Secondly, I felt they were totally misinterpreting the social mores of women as compared with men. They were giving an erroneous interpretation to that commanding officer. I said, "I don't blame the commanding officer one bit. That's your responsibility. Either give a clearance or not."

I said, "I'm going to support you in two ways. Either you court-martial these people or you give them a clearance. And I'll give you one week, because you know all the records. You've been over them 100 times. Or I'm going to the Secretary of the Navy." In one week, every, single one of them was cleared.

But this is the kind of thing I encountered, which was very demoralizing to me—to have to fight that kind of attitude, a very negative attitude. So I solved that one at least. That was one good point.

Paul Stillwell: Were many of these problems things that you had known previously, or did you get them in a turnover briefing with your predecessor?

Captain Collins: My predecessor was very ill, so I would say that was part of the problem.* No, I didn't get that kind of turnover. I found it out as I got into the job, more and more problems. And that's what I told Mr. Gates. I said the housing was miserable. I wanted to get the senior enlisted out on subsistence and quarters. The chief of the bureau would not authorize it. I said that the enlisted barracks, next to BuPers, was a tenement and, if I wouldn't get caught, I'd burn it down. Mr. Gates said, "I would like to see it." So you can imagine the flurry of the Secretary of the Navy coming over to inspect enlisted barracks. And the admirals were lined up behind him. He said to Admiral Smith, "I agree with Captain Quick. These are deplorable living conditions, and

---

* Captain Louise K. Wilde, USN, served as Assistant Chief of Naval Personnel for Women (Director of the WAVES) from 1953 to 1957. She reverted to the rank of commander when she was relieved, because the law at the time permitted only one Navy woman at a time to be a captain. In 1965 Wilde retired as a captain, her highest active duty rank.

I would like you to authorize subsistence and quarters for the chiefs and first class. And, of course, that relieved the housing there. It wasn't improved any, but it gave them more space.

Paul Stillwell: Was it a problem with overcrowding mostly?

Captain Collins: Yes, they were in cubicles and every space was taken. It was noisy. It was disruptive and—

Paul Stillwell: Not much privacy probably.

Captain Collins: Zero privacy. Zero recreation facilities. And the more senior, of course, were older, and it was very disturbing to them to have these young, noisy enlisted, just out of recruit training. Although I had pleaded very eloquently, I thought, to get them off substandard quarters, it was denied. Costs too much. It cost a pittance, really. So that's one example of Secretary Gates's support for me.

The other thing he said was, "There is no chain of command between your office and mine. If you have a problem you come directly. If anyone objects, let me know. I didn't take advantage of that, really, very often except in what I considered dire circumstances that I couldn't solve myself within the Navy. But it was nice to know I had that support there.

Paul Stillwell: Did you get any resentment from Admiral Smith that you were going around him on some of these things?

Captain Collins: He didn't realize I'd gone around, because the Secretary at the luncheon asked me the questions directly. So although I'd briefed him previously, in my initial call on him he asked a lot of questions and I told him very frankly the situation. And that's why he set it up in a very diplomatic way, so that no one would resent my going to him directly. And they never knew it.

Paul Stillwell: Did Smith ever warm up and become more cooperative?

Captain Collins: No, no, no. He just was interested in other things, including his promotions, as you've encountered many times.

Paul Stillwell: Had you ever had any contact with his predecessor Admiral Holloway?

Captain Collins: Oh, yes, yes.

Paul Stillwell: What was your assessment of Admiral Holloway?

Captain Collins: Oh, a board selected me, but he's the one who called in London and sent a confidential message. Oh, he was very outgoing, very warm, very cooperative with me. But he was there a very short time.

Paul Stillwell: He had been in BuPers several years before you arrived. Did you have any idea whether he had been supportive of women's programs?

Captain Collins: I think he lost respect for my predecessor in a sense, and so he—I can't answer that really. But I know there was great friction there because of what she did. But I had wonderful support from him. In fact, he had just lost his wife, and he was most empathetic to me. I became ill right after I'd been there, and I refused to go to the hospital. And he said, "I'll do your work."

I said, "Admiral, I hate to tell you, but you wouldn't know how." But we had a wonderful rapport and very supportive. But he left right away unfortunately.

He was really kind of shopping for a wife. And I was ducking. I teased young Jimmy once.* I said, "You know, but for fate, I could be your mother." But he was delightfully charming to me. He gave me luncheons and cocktail parties. And so it was a

---

* His son was Commander James L. Holloway III, USN, who was subsequently Chief of Naval Operations, 1974-78.

nice start for me in that regard. But I didn't get into the problems, of course, right off the bat, and by then he was gone.

Paul Stillwell: I see. What were some of the other things you had to tackle?

Captain Collins: Well, I told you recruitment was very bad. I found out that the recruiting organization received 100% if they met their quotas, but the women were not included in that. And it took me a whole year to get that changed. So then I started to get some results, because the finger was on the recruiters then, and they had to produce in terms of the women as well as the men. I don't know why that was never done before, because that's ridiculous. Naturally, they're not going to pay any attention or work hard unless they are included in their efficiency rating of the whole recruitment program. But these things take time to dig out. So most of the first year was demoralizing in terms of all the things that were wrong, as far as I was concerned.

Paul Stillwell: Did you provide any specific incentives to try to get more qualified women into the program?

Captain Collins: Oh, definitely. I picked topnotch women, enlisted and officers, to go into recruiting. First of all, they are an image. I worked out programs how they would go out into the colleges, high schools, add the team, a man and a woman. I wanted that image to be projected to the parents, that these were fine, nice-looking, clean-cut, young women, American women, so they could think of their daughter in terms of looking at this woman.

So we did not have the best candidates, in my opinion, in recruiting. That was one of the problems. The other was the recruiting program itself wasn't putting emphasis on them.

Paul Stillwell: Well, it is a non-traditional career for women. What selling points did you use on parents other than the clean-cut role models? What advantages could come to their daughters?

Captain Collins: Well, let me see. I did a study on what the women in the Navy thought of themselves, in terms of what kind of women join the Navy; if women are trained in the Navy and eventually get out, isn't this a waste of money? These are some of the questions that I had to answer in my own mind and that I was always being asked, policy-wise. When women do leave the Navy, do they find their experience in the Navy provides them with a better job in civilian life? These are some of the answers that I could give to parents and use in our publicity, our TV, our radio. Why should a woman think about a military career if she hopes to marry someday? How different are the jobs you have had in the Navy from what you could do as a civilian? What is meant by naval leadership? There's a tremendous gap there. The women's idea of themselves as a woman naval officer, enlisted, was very confused. They needed to find out that they are a very respectful person. And this is what I was digging at. And their image of themselves.

Paul Stillwell: That would apply to more than just recruiting. That would be boosting the morale of the people who were there already.

Captain Collins: Boosting the morale, but it reflected on recruiting by getting some of our top people. When I went around the country and talked to them, I found that there was a demoralized feeling of self, which had come about for many reasons. I mean, some of the men gave them problems. Some of the male leadership in the Navy didn't support them. So there were lots of reasons for it, and I was trying to dig it out and find out.

Then I started a whole leadership program in which they were compelled to attend these lectures. And it was highly successful, because they asked the questions about women in the Navy. "Why are we here? A lot of people don't like us." This kind of thing, see? So we dealt with it in a sense.

It also created esprit de corps among the women, that they came away with answers that they hadn't thought about themselves. I had some of the top male leaders in the Navy talk to them, and very supportive of them, and that kind of thing. And that was again reflected, of course, in recruiting and in job satisfaction, and everything.

Paul Stillwell: How did you measure that? Did you have a follow-up survey?

Captain Collins: From them, yes. To answer the questions that I asked and we talked about the problem of lesbianism, moral leadership, character, the difference between male standards and women's standards, both morally and all. And there was a distinct difference and always has been, of course. So we really dug into it, and then I had them fill out a questionnaire, answers to questions without signing their name, to give some idea of what they were thinking. So that helped to guide me.

But there was so much to do that I felt I'd never get half of this finished. But it was still enjoyable in the sense of step-by-step accomplishing something positive.

Paul Stillwell: The Navy has long had a very strict policy on homosexuality for men and women.

Captain Collins: Yes.

Paul Stillwell: How was that handled? I presume it was discreetly for the benefit of the individuals.

Captain Collins: Well, it isn't to the men, too discreetly. They're just dismissed if they confirm it.[*]

But the problem I had in the beginning was not proof, just suspect. And I insisted they either prove it, or clear them. And, of course, there was no excuse for the way they handled this, because these women had been in the Navy and they'd looked over their records so many times that it was preposterous, their treatment. And when I found out what they were doing, I just told them that in one week and that was it. And the head of

---

[*] This reflects the policy at the time of the interview in 1986. Shortly after the beginning of the administration of President Bill Clinton in 1993 came a new policy with regard to gays and lesbians in the military services. The policy did not openly condone homosexuality in the services; it maintained the traditional prohibition. Its "Don't ask, don't tell" provision dictated that the armed services would react only in response to overt evidence of homosexual activity rather than asking individuals to declare themselves gay or straight. In December 2010 Congress repealed the "Don't Ask, Don't Tell" regulation, thus opening the door for the gays and lesbians to serve openly.

performance said, "I'm going to take you to lunch. We're going to have a martini on that one."

But all these problems come up, and you have to figure out what is wrong. Why is this happening?

Paul Stillwell: Lack of understanding in that case.

Captain Collins: That's right, absolutely. If two men embrace, obviously, they're suspect. If two women do it, it's just normal for women to embrace, or to live together, and to socialize together, far more than men do, I think. So from that standpoint, they were misinterpreting actions of women. And I think we cleared that up pretty fast.

Paul Stillwell: You raised one question, among those you listed, the compatibility of marriage and a career for a Navy woman. How did you address that one?

Captain Collins: Well, we addressed it in this way. I got out a policy and got it approved for married Navy women. The Navy itself would make an effort to keep them with their spouses. So that was a great morale booster, because previously they were just separated. There was no effort by the detailers or anyone else in the Navy to try and keep a family unit together as best they could. Of course, when the man went to sea, there was no way that they could have the woman go to sea with him. But that was no different from a civilian wife. She was separated.

Paul Stillwell: So that really started during your tenure, a deliberate effort to—

Captain Collins: A delivered approved policy that there would be an effort made, and that was a great morale booster to the women.

Paul Stillwell: Well, and it got rid of a discouraging factor.

Captain Collins: It did. That's right, very much so.

Paul Stillwell: It would seem to me that another key to your boosting this image would be to get out more publicity on the kinds of jobs that women do in the Navy.

Captain Collins: Well, as a matter of fact, I did. And my first year, policy approval to permit married women, Navy women, to request assignment with spouse. That was a definite approved policy.

Then the Development of Leadership lectures, which I spoke to you about, geared to Navy women on character guidance and medical matters. Publication of career appraisal and role-playing material. Further development of career ladders for officers and enlisted women. We had no career ladder. I mean, they just went helter-skelter. But I developed a real career ladder by rank and by petty officer rating and what they had to do. Expansion of public relations program to use officer and enlisted in community programs. Expansion of TV and radio. And using some of the material that we gathered on this questionnaire about the career of the Navy woman and what she does and the kinds of jobs and self-image and all of that incorporated into that. So that was a positive step, no question.

Paul Stillwell: We talked before about the value of specific cases as an example. Do you recall any individual highlights of stories that you did bring to public attention?

Captain Collins: Well, part of what I found out from the public was the lack of knowledge about what women did in the Navy. Number one, what kinds of jobs, which educational requirements. If you have a sharp-looking young woman officer out there who is an outstanding college graduate and she can get up and talk to parents' groups, church groups, high schools, about the kinds of jobs she does. And also the enlisted woman on a high school level. So that they see the person, sharp looking, articulate, well informed. She tells where she lives, how she lives, what she does in her off-duty social time. Opportunities for education in the Navy for a woman were very important. From the parental standpoint, what kind of supervision is there? Very important. And so they were taught to get up and tell about that. How the chain of command works for women in terms of supervision.

One of the positive steps I took in the career ladder was to have certain jobs designated, "sea duty." These were the jobs in which a petty officer would be assigned as the CPO in a barracks.* They didn't volunteer for it until you put it in the career ladder. Then they could not get promoted unless they had that or had been at a recruit training command. So suddenly you get the best quality women trying to get these jobs, motivated instead of forcing them with a gun to go there. You also improve your leadership tremendously because you get topnotch people. So that was one of the things that was very productive.

I did the same thing for the women officers in the career ladder. They had to have had responsibility for women somewhere along the line; as an instructor, or in a district as the senior woman officer—we called her the commandant's representative. Any one of those they had to have when they came up for promotion. And that helped the whole system tremendously. It's like no man wants to go to sea just because he loves the sea.

Paul Stillwell: Well, I would disagree with that, but—

Captain Collins: Well, let's say that isn't the greatest motivating factor.

Paul Stillwell: Well, all right.

Captain Collins: Professionally, they know they must go to sea to attain higher rank.

Paul Stillwell: But many really enjoy it also.

Captain Collins: I know it. I know. I realize that. But what would happen if they just didn't have to do that for promotional reasons? You wouldn't have as many putting that down on their sheet, would you?

Paul Stillwell: Oh, I can agree with that, not as many.

---

* CPO – chief petty officer.

Captain Collins: Oh, some would.

I got the commanding officer for the recruit training, a woman, designated as commanding officer, which was shattering to some males in the Navy. They said that Navy regs wouldn't permit it. I said, "There is not the word 'she' in the whole book, I know." You know, it was ridiculous. But it was the attitude. Now we have many women commanding officers of all kinds of things. But that was a new idea. And all they were going to be was commanding officer for women, a separate command. But they deserved it. They were doing their jobs. So that was part of it.

Paul Stillwell: You've spoken of this matter of physical attractiveness, including the letter that went to London when they were trying to sell you over there.

Captain Collins: Yes.

Paul Stillwell: What do you do about the discrimination factor against someone who is very capable, but not especially attractive?

Captain Collins: Well, there are lots of jobs, but when you're going to put somebody in a showplace like recruiting, where we weren't getting the kind I wished, then you try and pick out somebody with physical and mental qualifications for that. One thing I did was I had a tremendous argument with BuMed in terms of weight standards.* Their weight standards were way above what the insurance companies were. I said, "I do not want fat women coming in the Navy." But I couldn't do anything about it as long as the standards were there. And finally, after many conferences and many arguments and getting the statistics from insurance companies to back me up, I had this captain call.

He said, "Well, the chief of BuMed has finally signed what you wanted. Now you can have all beanpoles." He was very much opposed. But from a public relations standpoint, I couldn't say, "You're overweight," to any of them if that was the BuMed standard. You see my point. And I couldn't send these little fatties out to represent us and try and get nice trim-looking young women.

---

* BuMed – Bureau of Medicine and Surgery.

So I put a tremendous emphasis on femininity in the Navy. I didn't want short hair. I got the high heels, pumps raised. And a mannish haircut was taboo. I said, "I like long, nice, pretty-looking hair," which made a difference. We had a great many women who had short-cropped hair and they looked like men, and it just didn't look good in a uniform in my opinion. Since I was the number one, why, I was going to have it my way if I could.

Paul Stillwell: Did you do anything to modify the uniform itself?

Captain Collins: Well, yes, I did. I told you we had a seersucker, which is the ugliest uniform. I call it the mattress cover. But, with the help of some designers, I came out with a blue uniform, striped blue, two piece, and it was very attractive.

Paul Stillwell: A light blue summer uniform.

Captain Collins: That's right. When I went before the Uniform Board, Admiral Smith was also head of the Uniform Board—and, of course, there was a tremendous number of males on that board. I set it up very cleverly. I had the prettiest girl I could find in the blue and not so pretty in the old gray. But fate interfered, and that morning, let's go to the board. The pretty girl was ill. I had about one hour to try and find a replacement.

Paul Stillwell: Her size too.

Captain Collins: That's right. The whole thing was a crisis for me. I thought I'd just do a nice snow job. Well, it didn't work that way. So Admiral Smith said, "Well, I can't understand why you want a new uniform. I think that young lady in that gray looks very attractive."

I thought, "Oh, boy, you would." Typical male reaction.

This would cost money, naturally, to change the uniform. And you have to have pretty sound reasons before you go to the Uniform Board. I said that it had been fleet tested and met all the requirements. I got input from the head of the Nurse Corps,

Captain Jackson, who was a very cooperative one.* So they had tested it, although, of course, the nurses don't wear it very much except on recruiting duty or something like that. But I had the full feminine contingent in the Navy approving this fleet tested, easy to care for, many qualities that the gray didn't have, which was miserable to care for. While they were arguing about it, one magnificent supply corps officer said, "Well, Admiral, there's another problem. We have yards and yards of that material on the shelves, the gray, but it is rotting."

I thought, "Oh, what a person." I didn't even know him. Oh, he certainly got a thank you from me. And he said, "In terms of cost, see, it will cost the same to replace the gray as it will the blue." Admiral Smith reluctantly agreed with me and approved it.

But those are some of the examples. It looks simple to get something like that through, but it isn't. You work very hard. I think I wouldn't have had much problem if I'd had that pretty, little girl there, because that's all he would have seen, not the facts I displayed in terms of the uniform and how the women liked it and the care and that it could be worn on shipboard. It could be worn around the world, anywhere. So that was one I won.†

Paul Stillwell: Well, and it should be a situation where you have to make a convincing case. If things are too easy, then the Navy would change willy-nilly.

Captain Collins: Yes, and there's a dollar sign always attached to these things. And we'd had this since 1942. It was thoroughly disliked. I thought it was an ugly uniform. It didn't look good in public. It didn't look like a uniform. It was a dress. And this other had military buttons and sharp looking, pale blue with stripes.

Paul Stillwell: Two-piece.

---

* Captain Wilma Leona Jackson, NC, USN, was Director of the Navy Nurse Corps from May 1954 to May 1958. Her oral history is in the Naval Intitute collection.
† The new summer uniform was approved in late 1957. For a photo of women wearing the new outfit, see Collins's memoir *More Than a Uniform*, page 173.

Captain Collins: Yes, and it would look well on most women's figures, not the fatties, but most.

And let's see, what else here? Well, I told you about expanding public relations. And then constantly looking for ways to improve the career opportunities. I got approval for postgraduate study for women officers in [unclear], comptrollership, personnel administration, business administration, communications engineering, naval intelligence, and Navy middle management. Those were new kinds of opportunities for women officers. And approval of a plan to permit enlisted women to qualify for commissions. That was a real battle with planning and BuPers. I had an Alabaman there who didn't know much about women, and he just objected. Although, compared to the enlisted men, which I did a study on—and Admiral Metcalf was in BuPers planning in those days.[*] He was very supportive of me.

But the enlisted man had—oh, I think I have the percentages down here—a high percentage—high school graduate was the top, very few college—whereas, with our women, 9% had one to four years of college. Eighty-two percent completed high school. Nine percent completed 5th to 11th of GED equivalent.[†] So we were a much better educated segment of enlisted personnel in the Navy. And yet they were barring their being commissioned. So I finally won that one. It wasn't easy. Admiral Smedberg was Chief of Bureau then.[‡] Admiral B. J. Semmes was the one who was so opposed.[§] And I said I would not stop. I was going to the bureau chief. And I'd very much like him to go with me if he would. And I knew he would. So when we got in there, he said, "You first."

I said, "Oh, no, no. You're senior. You go first." So he did. And he talked as though I really was making such a boo-boo, taking this beautiful WAVE officer corps.

I said, "They are not a corps." I was deliberately pushing these enlisted women to be commissioned.

---

[*] Lieutenant Joseph Metcalf III, USN. At the time of this interview he was a vice admiral serving as Deputy Chief of Naval Operations (Surface Warfare).
[†] The GED (general equivalency diploma) tests were a means of providing certification of high school-level education for those who had dropped out of school prior to graduation.
[‡] Vice Admiral William R. Smedberg III, USN, served as Chief of the Bureau of Naval Personnel from 12 February 1960 to 11 February 1964. His oral history is in the Naval Institute collection.
[§] Rear Admiral Benedict J. Semmes Jr., USN, who was serving in the Bureau of Naval Personnel. In 1964, after Captain Collins retired, he became chief of the bureau.

So Admiral Smedberg said, "Well, what do you say?"

I said, "Well, I have three records here of enlisted women. I'd like you to look them over." One had a master's, the other two were college graduates. And then I gave him these statistics, which I just gave you. And I said, "I see no reason why we should not permit women to be commissioned the same as the enlisted men are who aren't nearly as well qualified educationally."[*]

Paul Stillwell: So, really, it was an artificial bar. If they'd walked in off the street, they could have been commissioned.

Captain Collins: That's right, that's right. Well, they'd gone in during the war, because the officer program was closed, thinking that they'd get an opportunity. And they didn't. And I felt it wasn't right. Here they were well educated.

So gradually you open these doors.

Paul Stillwell: And that provides an incentive also for your top performing women, something for them to aspire to.

Captain Collins: Of course. That's right. Well, the educational program was a great success with the women officers. They didn't have this opportunity, because they were barred previously to go to any of these postgraduate courses.

Paul Stillwell: Were you able to upgrade the training opportunities for enlisted people?

Captain Collins: Yes, definitely. Approval of a plan to permit enlisted women to apply for commissions. Then the scientific educational program opened to enlisted women. That was just, at that point, just for men.

---

[*] Once he saw their records, Admiral Smedberg approved the commissioning of the three women and opened the door for more to follow. See *More than a Uniform*, pages 151-152.

Paul Stillwell: NESEP.*

Captain Collins: Yes. And increased emphasis on recruitment of enlisted women and qualified women officer candidates. And we increased the radio and TV and press presentations. I worked with recruiting in giving these kinds of facts, because parents wanted to know, and these were the kinds of things that applicants wanted to know. So that they had some preparation instead of just going out to recruiting and not knowing how to answer these questions. They would hit the questions head on. "This is what we do. This is where we live. This is where we work. This is the kind of thing. And here I am, you know, sharp-looking and so forth." So it was a very positive program.

The other thing was that promotion was a terrible problem. The reason it was a problem, promotion was based on only the regular Navy women, whereas the men were based on the regular Navy plus the reserve, which gives them a tremendous cushion. The law prohibited us from basing it on the reserve. And until we got the law changed, it was just miserable promotions.

Let's see, approval of women line, Supply Corps, augmentation program was not available at that time, but I got approval of that. So women below the rank of lieutenant could apply, both staff and line.

Paul Stillwell: Was there any other way of becoming a regular officer for a woman then except augmentation?

Captain Collins: That was the only way, but we didn't have that at first, so this was an emphasis which I got approved. Of course, everything had to be policy approved, as you well know.

Approval of women officers—commanders on lieutenant commander and commander boards. We never had a woman before. I felt it was very important that a woman be there to help interpret, because some of the men had never worked with women. They didn't know. And so that was a big step forward.

---

* NESEP—Navy Enlisted Scientific Education Program, which is no longer in existence. Under its provisions the Navy paid for the college education of promising enlisted personnel, then sent them through the Officer Candidate School for training and commissioning as officers.

Paul Stillwell: Even now there's contention about the language used in fitness reports for men and women.

Captain Collins: That's right, yes.

Paul Stillwell: Was that a thing that you addressed?

Captain Collins: No, I wasn't trying to address that so much, because that would be impossible to control. What I wanted was a well-qualified senior woman officer there, who could consult with the men about the fitness reports and interpret them to them. And they'd be comparing one woman against another. Now we have a selection of women with the men so they are compared on the same basis, but we didn't have that then.

But a woman there could do a really fine job on the selection board in assisting, interpreting, so that they just didn't pick them by somebody saying, "She's very attractive." What kinds of jobs they were doing, the importance of the job, and so forth. Because many of the men knew the seagoing jobs very well, but they didn't always know the shore jobs as well. So that was a great help in getting the quality they wanted promoted.

Paul Stillwell: Well, also, people develop a service reputation and women might be more likely to know the service reputations of these people.

Captain Collins: That's right, yes. They would.

The other one was approval of and selection of enlisted women for five-term program to get their degrees. That was important for morale purposes. Expansion of enlisted regular strength to almost 5,000. And the reserve, an increase in that too. An annual quota of 100 officers per year. And I was having trouble meeting it.

Paul Stillwell: Why so?

Captain Collins: Some of these things I talked about: public attitude, military male attitude, the fact that recruiting wasn't compelled to have a quota for women and fill it. That was a big thing. They just weren't bothering. They were busy getting their 100% on all other items of their quota, and so why should they take time for this one when it didn't count on their rating? So when I found out that, why, I got that changed. And that made a tremendous difference.

Paul Stillwell: That really seems like a small number now.

Captain Collins: Doesn't it? Oh, yes. But imagine that small number like that and you not meeting even that. In fact, it got so low that [telephone interruption]. Where was I?

Paul Stillwell: We were talking about increasing the number of women officers recruited.

Captain Collins: Oh, yes, yes.

Paul Stillwell: Did you succeed in meeting the goal after it was put in as a specific incentive?

Captain Collins: About my third year, I did. Before that it got so bad, I only had nine officers to go to a class at Newport.[*] I didn't need anybody to tell us that we couldn't afford to have a staff up there for nine people. So I called the head of the Nurse Corps, and I said, "By any chance, would you like your women officers who've just come in the Navy to go to our indoctrination school.

She says, "I'd be thrilled to death." And that saved my neck really. Because their recruiting was going very well for Nurse Corps. And I thought it was a splendid idea aside from my need. This would give them a chance to get acquainted with one another, and the Nurse Corps never had any indoctrination, as the doctors don't today. And so it

---

[*] Newport, Rhode Island, was the site of Officer Candidate School.

was a highly successful program, and she was thrilled to death for it. So the school stayed open.

Paul Stillwell: What was the relationship between the Nurse Corps and the WAVES? Were the nurses not considered part of the WAVES?

Captain Collins: No, no, no way. I would say it was not good, not bad. They just didn't know each other. But this did provide a tremendous bond between them, which was very good for morale purposes. Because they would meet from time to time. And the captain of the Nurse Corps was thrilled to death with the change in attitudes. They knew about the Navy. They knew how to salute. They were well informed. Their morale was high. It really boosted their morale tremendously, because then they felt were a part of the regular Navy.

Paul Stillwell: What was included in the curriculum at Newport for women officer candidates?

Captain Collins: The same as men; history, ships and aircraft, leadership, protocol, etiquette, history.

Paul Stillwell: They probably wouldn't get as much of specific seagoing skills like navigation, though, would they?

Captain Collins: They'd get some, yes, recognition of ships and aircraft and that kind of thing and not necessarily the operational knowledge. They didn't go into that. But still, it gave them a common background, which was very helpful to them when they went out into the Navy.

Paul Stillwell: Well, and even for a nurse, being able to converse in a patient's language would help.

Captain Collins: That's right, tremendous. It was a great morale boost for them.

Paul Stillwell: Well, did you then keep that going for all subsequent nurses?

Captain Collins: Yes, I think it's still going. I don't know. I believe it is. Because it was so successful, from the individual's point of view as well as from the policy point of view up above.

Let's see. Oh, I changed the obligation for enlisted women from four to three years, which did help recruiting a great deal. Four years to a young woman seemed like a lifetime. And so that was one of the techniques I used and got approved to reduce that, and it helped our recruiting immeasurably. Sounds simple, but it isn't that simple.

Paul Stillwell: Did you increase the number and types of jobs that women were eligible to fulfill?

Captain Collins: Oh, yes, constantly, constantly seeking opportunities both educationally and kinds of jobs and include them in the career pattern so that jaygees do this and lieutenants do this the same as they do for the men. But seeking new kinds of more responsible jobs all the way along. The uniform change approval for enlisted women in pay grades E-7 and above to wear the dark blue, officer-type—that was a great morale boost.* They wanted the same kinds of uniforms as the men had. I had to go before the Uniform Board and plead that and, again, they couldn't see why they wanted it. I said, "Well, they do." And of course, they would pay for it. This wasn't out of the pockets of the Navy at all. I remember one case. I guess it was out at Moffett Field, when I was speaking to all of the women.† One chief said, "Captain, I don't see why we have to pay for these uniforms."

I said, "Every one of you told me you wanted them."

"Oh, yes, we wanted them."

---

* These are the Navy's top three enlisted pay grades: E-7, chief petty officer; E-8, senior chief petty officer; E-9, master chief petty officer.
† Moffett Field Naval Air Station, Sunnyvale, California, was located ten miles north of San Jose, at the southern tip of San Francisco Bay.

And I said, "By the way, do you have a car?"

She said, "Yes."

I said, "What model is it?" She told me and it was that year. And I said, "Well, I tell you what you do. You just dig right down in your little pocket and pay for it." Because, I mean, she had a brand-new, expensive car and they'd begged me. And I just knocked myself out to get this uniform, and then she was griping. Well, of course, they all laughed at her then. That was it. But it's known that you can't please everyone.

Paul Stillwell: That's right.

Captain Collins: But I was trying to do the best I could for all of them, and this was what they said they wanted. So I went to bat for them. And they had to pay for it, as the men had to pay for it. There was no difference in that, whatsoever.

Paul Stillwell: Did you make that argument also?

Captain Collins: Oh, definitely. I said, "You wanted it. You knew you were going to have to pay for it, and now you're griping about it." And that's when I used the example of her car. And the others just laughed at her then.

They said, "That's the end of it." Humor is a great help.

Paul Stillwell: The concept of ombudsman has become very popular. Did you have something of that sort on your staff to field gripes and deal with specific problems?

Captain Collins: No, I got them all. I wasn't that far advanced. My staff was very small; I had a deputy and three enlisted. But one thing I did do was have women's representatives throughout the bureau in detailing, enlisted and officer, and plans. I made arrangements with the head of each division that I would give a collateral fitness report. They were the eyes and ears, and I'd have a staff meeting with these women once a week. So I was trying to spread some of the leadership role, policy role to these women and to their bosses. So that worked pretty well. Because otherwise I wasn't rewarding them for the work they did, and they weren't getting recognition from their bosses of the work they were doing with me, which I felt in fairness to them was very important.

Paul Stillwell: You had a good example last time you talked about Captain Mack and his role as the commander detailer. Did you stay in frequent touch with the detailers to see that women were getting good jobs?

Captain Collins: Oh, yes, that was the job of the woman in personnel, Pers-B, detailing. She detailed all women, but she did it, coordinating it with the various kinds of desks. We had rank desks, and then we also had command desks for all the commands. So she worked with all those. And that was a highly successful program, because she personally knew all these people and could go and talk to them about a record. And it was a personal sales job always.

Paul Stillwell: Well, as it is for the men, too. You try to match the person to the job.

Captain Collins: Yes, that's right. But, you see, they weren't used to having women in a lot of these jobs, and so she was really the prime sales person.

Paul Stillwell: It helps to have somebody aggressive in that job.

Captain Collins: I tried to pick them that way. With a nice personality, who'd get along well, and that's how they got the jobs really.

Well, I told you about the development of a career pattern for enlisted women to parallel, quote, sea duty.

Paul Stillwell: Was there any talk of women actually getting sea duty at that point?

Captain Collins: Well, they had the MSTS.* They had that. That's all. And of course, that was civilian dependents—an awful lot of them on those ships. But that's the only

---

* MSTS – Military Sea Transportation Service, a part of the Navy that operated ships for support functions.

sea duty they could have. The law prohibited it in any other than a dependent ship pretty much. It was a legal restriction. Until that was changed, we couldn't do anything about it.*

Paul Stillwell: Did you make any attempts to bring it toward what it is now that there are more ship types that women can go aboard?

Captain Collins: No, I had enough problems just with the shore billets. We weren't getting the kinds of more responsible jobs we should have, in my opinion. I was constantly seeking those kinds of jobs. I would personally talk to the commanders' desks and identify the kinds of jobs that women could hold, which were more responsible. It's a gradual process and a lot of it depends on the person in that commander job. So it's a persuasive one definitely.

Paul Stillwell: Well, and if she does well, she's accepted in her command, and if not they find a way to work around her.

Captain Collins: That's right, yes. If she does well, then others will in that command. They want more. That's ever so. But, see, a lot of it was having a woman be successful in a new kind of job. That was it. Always a new experience. And then they found that a woman could do an awful lot of things, but they didn't think so, you see, until they tried it out. So it was an uphill persuasion always.

Oh, yes, I had another problem in that two agents would interrogate, say, an enlisted woman who was possibly thought of as being a lesbian. And so many of them were so young, they didn't even know what the word meant. I had an inkling that something was very wrong in their interrogation. So I finally got BuPers manual modified to require that a woman officer be present at any interrogation. Oh, and they fought me tooth and nail about it. They said I'd interfere with them.

I said, "She won't say a word.

---

* Subsequent to this interview, in 1992 the Defense Authorization Act repealed the long-standing combat-exclusion law for women pilots in the Navy and Air Force. In 1993 President Bill Clinton signed a bill that ended the combat exclusion for women on board combatant ships.

She's just going to be present." But the dismissals just dropped like that. Because they were using awful strong-arm tactics on these young kids and they didn't do anything wrong. Very few lesbians really.

Paul Stillwell: They were intimidated by the process.

Captain Collins: Scared to death. Two male agents, you know, hammering, "We've seen you holding hands with a girl. What is it?" They just gave up, signed a statement. But when a woman officer was there, no way. Statistics just proved that my theory was right. I said, "You're intimidating them." And of course, that's a costly thing to train a person from the Navy standpoint, and a recruit crew will then get rid of them. No way. That isn't the way it should be. You should go in and find out what's wrong.[*]

Then I also revised the homosexuality lecture for training schools, because I felt that they weren't giving sufficiently in-depth kinds of lectures about the subject, that they need to discuss it fully. Particularly the young recruits needed to know what homosexuality was and beware of it in a sense, but also just to know what it is. Many of them didn't even know about it. So that was part of the program.

Then I redefined the responsibilities of the women who were assistant to the commandants or assistant to commanding officers—to define their role in terms of supervision of women as his arm in that regard. And many of the commanding officers said, "I don't know what this woman is supposed to do." So I just got busy and wrote it down with their approval. And I sent it out, preliminary, to several commanding officers that I knew very well and said, "You see if this meets your needs, and if not, add what you think we should." And so it came out pretty well. That also was good for the woman in that job, because she really didn't know what she was supposed to do except what the commanding officer told her. And that's no way to run anything.

Paul Stillwell: A CO might wonder, "How do I know what to tell her?"

---

[*] This is now a moot point. Since 2011 homosexuals have been allowed to serve openly in the U.S. Armed Forces.

Captain Collins: That's right. And many of them didn't know what to say. They just gave it all to her and said, "You do it." And many of them were scared of disciplining women. And so this defined that they should have discipline for women the same as for men, very distinct, no difference, whether they cried or didn't cry. And that's why a woman officer was very good there. That was spelled out, and commanding officers were tremendously pleased about that.

On the enlisted side, I initiated a leadership program. That's when the Navy had an overall leadership program, and I got about six enlisted women to work with the male leadership teams. They went around the country to provide leadership for enlisted women and improve image of self and all these things, and all the things enlisted women couldn't answer, and what's wrong and what's right. And that was very successful.

Paul Stillwell: Secretary Gates was big on the idea of moral leadership.[*]

Captain Collins: Oh, yes.

Paul Stillwell: So that tied in with what you were doing.

Captain Collins: Yes, he's a terrific person. I wanted him to be president. We became great friends. I used to see him quite a bit socially when he was Secretary of Defense.[†] He just died last year.[‡]

Paul Stillwell: There's a new ship being named for him.

Captain Collins: Yes, but oh, he was a wonderful leader. One of the men on the CPC board with me was from Philadelphia, and he knew him very well.[§] He went to the funeral, and he said the grandson gave the most beautiful eulogy he'd ever heard for

---

[*] On 17 May 1958 Secretary of the Navy Thomas S. Gates issued General Order Number 21 to all ships and stations on the subject of leadership.
[†] Thomas S. Gates, Jr., served as Secretary of Defense from 2 December 1959 to 20 January 1961.
[‡] Gates died 25 March 1983. The keel for the guided missile destroyer *Thomas S. Gates* was laid at Bath Iron Works on 31 August 1984, and the ship was commissioned 22 August 1987.
[§] After her retirement from the Navy, Collins was on the board of CPC, which had previously been known as the Corn Products Refining Company. She discussed that experience later in the oral history.

anyone. And I thought that sounds as though his leadership has carried over. Did you ever know him personally?

Paul Stillwell: No, I didn't, but so many people have talked about him and in terms similar to those you use.

Captain Collins: Well, you can see how I was devoted to him, because he really helped my morale so much in that I knew I had somebody there if I really got to the point I couldn't handle it.

Paul Stillwell: Well, and another distinction that people have drawn is that he was not the typical political appointee just putting in time.

Captain Collins: No way.

Paul Stillwell: He had the knowledge. He did his homework, and he was interested in what was best for the Navy.

Captain Collins: Well, he was tremendously interested in people. That was the only barracks he ever inspected in his total career, but it was really just unbelievable to some of the admirals that he would take the time to do that. That's the kind of man he was. He was very interested in the enlisted and the officer. He wanted the Navy to be a bright spot for them career-wise. And I would say he's a great moral leadership man himself, by his example.

Paul Stillwell: Right.

Captain Collins: I told you I made a career pattern for the enlisted program. Evaluating new programs and billets which are suitable for enlisted all the way along. And I opened the nursing education program to women hospital corpsmen in which they could get their four years of nursing education, four years of college free.*

The other one was improving the living conditions for enlisted women, which were deplorable, I thought. And I got a number of barracks converted so that instead of the partitions, they became rooms. And now the Navy has adopted that for all enlisted personnel, but that was a new idea then. It wasn't that much more expensive, but it was a tremendous improvement in morale, because of the noise and all of that that goes with mass living.

Paul Stillwell: There was one of these rhetorical questions that you asked early. What about the fact that the Navy invests time and money in women and then they go on out into civilian life? How did you answer that one?

Captain Collins: Well, I did a study of the number of men discharged for various reasons, and there wasn't a whole lot of difference. Part of the reason that we had a little higher was because of marriage, but then I studied whom they married. And so I pretty well could answer that. I said, "You're getting two for one when they marry in the Navy. And she's already trained and she knows about the whole Navy system, so she's going to be a very supportive wife." But actually in discharge numbers, I was surprised. I thought it would be much higher for enlisted women. That's one of the reasons I had it changed from four to three years, for recruitment reasons. But actually, it wasn't that much different. The men always said, "Oh well, you have such a high attrition." I didn't know whether we did or not. But I did the study on the women, and then I did the study on the men so I could talk from knowledge.

They didn't know either. I could say, "No, that isn't so." I said, "It's very small."

Paul Stillwell: Well, it's just an assumption really.

---

* Hospital corpsman is a Navy enlisted rating, that is, an occupational specialty.

Captain Collins: That's right. And they were trying to tell me it's much more expensive to have women in the Navy, because all they do is come in and then they get married, see. And I said, "Also, men get out for many kinds of reasons."

I don't think we ever had AOL women, never.* Men, you have a high percentage AOL. I had all those statistics, which was an illumination to me definitely. But I got an awful lot of flak on that, so one day I asked the performance people if they could make a study for me and break it down as to the reasons the men left and so forth. Principally, it was pregnancy with marriage. I mean marriage and/or pregnancy, that women left. But not discipline cases, very few. Whereas the men, that's a lot of it.

Paul Stillwell: Well, even for people who complete their enlistments and choose not to make a career, Admiral Burke had an answer that the Navy is here to serve the society, and one way it serves it is by training people to do better once they get to civilian life.

Captain Collins: That's true and, of course, they do, because they get magnificent training in a four-year or six-year period. They get to go to the advanced schools. And many of them in certain fields are just grabbed by employers, so that isn't a loss to society. It's expensive to the Navy, granted, but it is not a loss to the nation, as such.

Paul Stillwell: That's exactly the point he was making.

Captain Collins: Yes, that's right. I agree with him completely.

Let's see. I tried some other uniform items. Hat tops were a mess. They had to be washed. I got the vinyl, which was easy to care for. Enlisted women had dungaree slacks, which I abhorred. See I was way, way out of step with what came along with the Levi's. But I got those out of the uniform, and I had very chic-looking slacks. I still can't stand dungarees on women, but—

Paul Stillwell: Well, they're not as flattering as these designer jeans.

---

* AOL – absent over leave.

Captain Collins: And these were polyester slacks, and they looked much better. So I got rid of the darn dungarees.

Paul Stillwell: It's amazing as you recount these, the range of things that you were involved in, from the very high level down to specific things.

Captain Collins: I was, oh, the whole works. And most of them were problems.

Paul Stillwell: Well, if they hadn't been problems, they would've been solved somewhere else.

Captain Collins: That's right, that's right.

Oh, and again, this was in '61, I was pushing to have the active reserves be counted with the active regulars. I did get a revision on restriction on the upper grades to permit determination to be made administratively by the Secretary of the Navy before we had to do it within BuPers. It was at 10 and 20% and that was it. But there was no variation.

Paul Stillwell: What do you mean by "10 and 20%?"

Captain Collins: Well, that was of the total number of regular women in the Navy, only 20% could be lieutenant commanders and 10%, commanders. But if I had it determined administratively by the Secretary of the Navy, I could fudge one year where we maybe had a bigger group to be considered, and lowered the next. In other words, it gave some flexibility and also was a tremendous morale booster, because under the old rules, a woman could be considered five times and not make it. Not through any fault of her own, but because of the numerical restrictions. The legislation didn't get changed on my watch, but it ultimately did. And you know how long it takes to get legislation changed.

I recommended legislation change that placed active duty reserve officers before the same selection board as regulars, so we could have some comparable standards.

Well, a study of the many laws that we had regarding retirement, statutory retirement age, retirement pay, and all of that.

Paul Stillwell: Was there any change when the Kennedy Administration came in?[*] Was Secretary Connally supportive and helpful?[†]

Captain Collins: Yes, he was, very. I liked Connally. He was very outgoing, very positive, and every year I set out goals.

And of course, one of them was constantly increasing the career opportunities at enlisted and officer level.

Then I encouraged the Supply Corps to develop career patterns for Supply Corps women. They didn't have anything. They were designated supply, and they just went from job to job, but no progression.

And educating all Navy personnel regarding what the career patterns for women were.

Oh, great emphasis on the women reservists regulars who'd come in to get them to augment, because the more numbers I had, the more promotions I had. So there was great stress put on that.

Paul Stillwell: Was there a ceiling on the number of regular women that could be in the Navy?

Captain Collins: The law was 500 at that time. But we weren't near that, so that wasn't a problem. It was to build up the base.

I did considerable on the administration of women to define the senior woman's role in all of the commands. And this was formally defined in CNO and BuPers regulations.[‡]

---

[*] John F. Kennedy served as President of the United States from 20 January 1961 until he was assassinated on 22 November 1963.
[†] John B. Connally Jr., served as Secretary of the Navy from 25 January 1961 to 20 December 1961.
[‡] CNO – Chief of Naval Operations.

I told you about the BuPers organizational charts. I had the functions of the women liaison officers spelled out, so it was an official kind of job, attached to each of the divisions, but liaison to my office.

Preparation of training manuals for the chiefs who had the master at arms duties to know their responsibilities and what they were supposed to do. We never had anything like that. They just went into the job, and some did well and some did lousy.

Then I had a course of instruction, which I arranged for them to come to Quarters K for a two-weeks training program. I had qualified masters at arms go through and teach them, which, of course, helped them a great deal as well as their general performance of duty in the field.

Paul Stillwell: Was Quarters K the one that you mentioned earlier?

Captain Collins: Yes, that's the one where all the Washington enlisted women stayed.

Then I had an officer candidate program in which I had a study and reappraisal of the selection standards used in selecting women officers, including tests, interviews, records, recommendations, motivation, and attitudes, to find out what was good and what was bad and what we needed more of and so forth.

Then I had a study to do a reappraisal of the ratings in which enlisted women could be utilized beyond what they were at that time.

Reappraisal of the assignment of women seamen to class A schools. Is the percentage of qualified women adequate? Usually we had more qualified than were getting into that narrow little eye of the needle, so this was motivating.

I developed opportunities for enlisted women to obtain commission status in the Medical Service Corps. The men were going in. The women weren't allowed. LDO and warrant, I got all that approved finally.

So it opened quite a few more opportunities for women to get commissions, which was only right in terms of the male.

Then I expanded the nursing education, which was four years of college to become nurses, to all enlisted ratings, not just the hospital corps.

Let's see. Reduction of disciplinary cases. Comparative percentage per year by type of discharge. I constantly tried to keep my eye on why we were losing people, what they're going out for and so forth, because in some ways that reflected on recruiting too. Maybe there was some reason why they weren't measuring up.

Paul Stillwell: Did you see the results of the leadership program in reduced number of discharges?

Captain Collins: Well, not so much in discharge as in morale, very definitely. Our discharges really weren't bad, except for those two reasons I told you. But we had very few disciplinary cases.

Paul Stillwell: Did you see the number drop during your tenure?

Captain Collins: I saw morale improve is what I'm talking about. The discipline problems were minimum for both officer and enlisted. But morale was a tremendously bad factor when I first came into it. It was very demoralizing to me.

I'd been in London. I didn't know what was going on. And I really tried to hit that head on in every way I could think of, because unless people respect themselves in any kind of a job, they're not going to do a good job. And also they didn't know how to answer criticisms of women in the Navy. A lot of them didn't know why they were in the Navy, frankly. Why should we have women in the Navy? That's a good question. If you're a woman in the Navy, and you don't believe in that or don't know the reasons they're there, it affects your morale, particularly if some enlisted man says, "We shouldn't have women in the Navy." That kind of thing. So the leadership program was tremendous in that regard. It gave answers and it found out problems, both ways. Then we tried to work out the problems to help morale, and make them more efficient and more responsible. Be proud of themselves in uniform and all these other factors.

Paul Stillwell: Were there cases in which women officers were not treated with the respect that men officers were?

Captain Collins: Oh, lots of cases, I'm sure. But you'd try to identify one, and I know in some cases I went to the commanding officer and I said, "I think the men need some leadership training in these kinds of things." So that was also a plus, because we have laws now that don't permit that kind of discrimination, and we didn't have them then. And so there was the harassment and the whistling and that kind of thing, which can be very demoralizing to women. Once a commanding officer understood that, most of them were very cooperative in getting at that problem.

Paul Stillwell: Well, it's a matter of education, really.

Captain Collins: That's right, yes.

I also designed a formal uniform, because we did not have anything previously. It was a nice jacket with a short or a long dress and a tiara, which all the press liked and all the senior women liked.* The only ones that were required were the commanders, and it was optional for the others. But it was very attractive and very feminine and it looked good. The men loved it.

Let's see—directives regarding the appearance in civilian clothes on active duty. Immaculate grooming. I said they'd never get on report for long hair. They'd get on report for short hair.

But civilian clothing was a problem for some women. They just picked out miserable clothes, and so we tried to give examples—the kinds of clothes they should wear as a civilian. That's no problem for a man, although some of them are pretty sloppy in their civilian clothes too. But it isn't the same kind of problem. There's such a range of clothing for women.

Increased emphasis on diet, personal grooming, appropriate leisure clothing for enlisted women. I got some attractive shorts for them to wear; white shorts, white shirts. It made a nice appearance.

Paul Stillwell: Were there guidelines on conduct during off-duty hours?

---

* This uniform was approved in early 1962. See Collins's memoir *More Than a Uniform*, pages 175-176.

Captain Collins: Definitely, yes, absolutely.

Reappraisal of all the publicity. Devise more effective means for reaching eligible juniors and seniors in college, starting with the juniors. Find out what the coeds felt about the Navy, what were their objections, what were their false impressions, and answer those. And we increased publicity tremendously. Radio, in the colleges, interviews, speaking engagements.

Paul Stillwell: What were the big selling points to encourage women to join the Navy? Travel, responsibility?

Captain Collins: Well, one little thing I used to do as a humorous thing at the end of it was just that it's the only occupation which is 99.44% men. Which, you know, is a great appeal. It was a humorous comment, but it's true.

Paul Stillwell: It registers.

Captain Collins: Oh, definitely. And giving them examples of what the social life was like. Because that's what they think of. They all want to get married, and they all want a boyfriend. And so, unless you approach it from their point of view of that, you're not going to get them.

Paul Stillwell: There are some very specific rules now on fraternization between officers and enlisted. Was that a factor back then?

Captain Collins: Yes, it always has been. It was a factor. An officer couldn't take an enlisted to an officer club. They obviously went out with them, but so long as they weren't discrediting or becoming obviously a problem, why, it was all right.

Paul Stillwell: Was there a rule against it occurring in the same chain of command?

Captain Collins: That was up to the commanding officer, as he spelled it out. Because I feel that was his prerogative. We shouldn't dictate. But it was felt that fraternization would be the same as it was for enlisted men and vice versa, enlisted man and a woman officer. It goes both ways.

One of the things was constant emphasis that only the finest young women come into the service, and point it out in so many different ways; appearance, education, opportunities, social life, moral standards, character building, all of that. That was tremendously important to get the right kind of women coming into the service.

Paul Stillwell: Who really would make the decision on whether a specific individual could or could not join the Navy? Would that be the individual recruiter?

Captain Collins: Well, of course, the standards were there. They had to pass intelligence tests. They had to have interviews. They had to have their character checked in the community, in the school. Their moral character was strongly emphasized, more strongly for women than for men. Because I felt that was an important ingredient in their being successful and in creating the image, back to the community, of the kind of women we have in the service.

Paul Stillwell: So it would be up to the recruiter to say, "Yes, you do," or, "No, you don't," meet these standards?

Captain Collins: Well, not just the recruiter, the officer in charge. It would go to the officer in charge.

That would be the preliminary. After the test, the motivation of the individual was very important. "Why do you want to go in the service?" See? And when they knew about the opportunities, a lot of them just couldn't believe the kind of opportunities compared to civilian life, which weren't that plentiful for women, and still aren't. They're better, but . . .

Oh, increased emphasis on the internal public relations within the Navy. I found there was a tremendous lack of understanding. Articles in *All Hands*.[*] An appeal to the commanding officers everywhere I went that all personnel knew why women were in the Navy, the kind of women who were in the Navy, and what kinds of jobs they did. There was a total lack of information. And so that was a great help for the morale of women.

I worked with the Chaplain Corps in all of their magazines. We had articles about women in the Navy, because the parents, they're very much interested in that. And it was an education for a lot of the chaplains to get with it. But I had great cooperation from the Chaplain Corps.

Paul Stillwell: Well, another thing that strikes me as a possible morale builder would be selling the idea to women that they are elite, that it's a very selective group.

Captain Collins: That's right, only the finest, was always the emphasis to come in the Navy. That's why at recruiting level we emphasized the character and moral reputation of the individual far more than the man. Because we felt that would be a discredit to have a woman who didn't have good character.

We developed a Navy film indicating the leadership role of women in the Navy. That was a great idea. It improved public relations.

And increase national coverage. We really expanded that in all kinds of Navy publications. I'd interest one of the editors—and, of course, I met them all the time—in doing a story on a new kind of job for women. Well, of course, then that depicted the kind of woman she was, what women were doing in the Navy and the whole thing. But it was a national publicity.

Through the local community where a young woman would come in, I'd try to get them to write back a story to the editor, and so forth. And that was successful.

Paul Stillwell: Did you have any success on television?

---

[*] *All Hands* is a monthly magazine published by the Bureau of Naval Personnel.

Captain Collins: Yes, quite a bit, yes. I used the Navy League a lot for that—of getting them to sponsor a woman, enlisted or officer, and get TV coverage for her so she could tell about what she's doing in the Navy and how much she's enjoying it and where she's been and the kind of education she's getting. Radio, too, and newspapers. The hometown newspapers didn't have any stories on women in the Navy in the beginning. And they really worked with me beautifully. So that's where you get your good recruits, as you know.

Encouraged women on active duty to belong to civic organizations in the community and to offer to speak to parents and teachers' groups. And write back and tell me what they did and what it was, and then that would go out to others and so forth.

To collect and have duplicated and distributed personal interest stories concerning women in the Navy. A clearinghouse for wider exchange of ideas, recruiting practices and problems for women officers.

Establish a women liaison officer with all colleges, the graduates of those being ideal. Coed and non-coed, both. Arrange for preferably a recruiting woman officer to talk at NROTC programs to give them information and handouts regarding women in the Navy.*

Paul Stillwell: There was not yet at that point, was there, an opportunity for women to become regular officers through NROTC?

Captain Collins: No, I'm trying to think when that came in. I think it came in just about then, around '60-'61.

Paul Stillwell: So that must have been one of the programs that you buzzed through also.

Captain Collins: Yes, that's right.

---

* NROTC – Naval Reserve Officers' Training Corps, a program that provides training leading to officer commissions at selected universities.

Paul Stillwell: And that's another great incentive in that a woman can get her college education paid for.

Captain Collins: Absolutely, that's right.

Turning to '61 now. Career projects, promotional opportunities, pushing on the need for legislative relief to permit the active reserve to be counted on our numbers, which ultimately was done, but not on my watch.

Possibility for increasing the time of active commissioned service before becoming eligible for augmentation. That was to give a better review of the individuals.

For the officers to develop new jobs with increased executive responsibilities, taking in mind any PG work they had attained.

Attempt to obtain at least one billet per year at armed forces staff colleges. Provide for early rotation of junior officers within communications, because once the commanding officer got them in communications, they wanted them to stay forever.

Increase number of overseas billets for jaygees, in particular, lieutenants.

Paul Stillwell: Was there any push during your tenure to get women into the Naval Academy?

Captain Collins: I tried to get instructors there at that time. And Admiral Smedberg just thought the sky would fall if I did such a thing as that. He turned me down. They were sending men to postgraduate work to get advanced degrees in mathematics. I came back at him with about ten folders of qualified women, and a couple of them had Ph.Ds. The women in the Navy were highly educated—postgraduate, a tremendous number. He just thought it would be a terrible thing. I looked at him and I said, "Well, women have been teaching them all their lives. Why would this be so different?" I didn't win that one until later. Now they have a lot of them up there, of course, as you know.

Paul Stillwell: Well, and in the Bancroft Hall organization, too, the disciplinary setup.*

Captain Collins: Oh, yes, that's right. But that was too new for Smeddy, although he was very cooperative with me. And I really am very fond of him personally, but that was one he couldn't buy. He said, "I don't what they'd do to me. I'd probably be court-martialed." Isn't that funny when you think back on it—that negative attitude?

Paul Stillwell: Well, it takes somebody with some courage to break against the tradition.

Captain Collins: It does. That's right. Well, I broke quite a few. I said, "Develop opportunities for women officers as instructors at the U.S. Naval Academy and in the postgraduate school at Monterey. I got them into Monterey. This is '61. But I couldn't get Smeddy to go along.

Investigate feasibility of additional exchange of women officers with foreign countries and get them on NATO staffs, which I did.

Work closely with the women officers on BuPers leadership team.

Develop career and augmentation program for medical service women officers. Now, once they get in sometimes then medical service is a closed organization. Very few of them were male college graduates at all. Now I think their standards are up quite a bit. In those days it used to be ex-hospital corps with no college. That's part of what's wrong with the hospitals, I guess.

They have their share of problems—more than their share.

Captain Collins: They do, but part of it is the administration, very definitely. I have a lot of good doctor friends out there and they say it's absolutely unbelievable. Fifty percent of their time is spent on administration. And they really want to treat patients.

Paul Stillwell: Sure.

---

* Bancroft Hall is the large multi-wing dormitory that houses Naval Academy midshipmen. It also contains the offices of members of the executive department, including the commandant, executive officer, and battalion and company officers.

Captain Collins: In terms of enlisted women, I established a course of professional development for enlisted women for advancement to E-8 and E-9.

Increase the number of seamen apprentice attending Class A schools.* For those not attending class A schools, increase on the job training at command level. Use of off-duty classes in special studies. Enlist aid to assure that women seamen are preparing themselves for advancement. Reappraise the ratings in which enlisted women may be utilized and expand it. Increase opportunities in those grades for which there is no Class A school. Ensure that enlisted women are receiving training and that technical ratings be used in those ratings. If they go to school and then not be used in it, I felt it was a terrible misuse of Navy funds and the individual.

Decrease attrition at Class A schools, particularly in the technical training, by emphasizing qualifications in the beginning and work with recruit training to ensure greater emphasis on classification process. More broadened education for seamen recruits on what is involved. Continue effort to open new opportunities for enlisted women, including independent duty for more senior petty officers. Previous to this we had to always send a group. We couldn't just send one. And when they're a senior petty officer, why not?

Screen carefully those women selected for leadership roles, both enlisted, master at arms, and the recruit-training program and recruiting and the leadership teams. Those were the key spots for the topnotch people.

Opportunity for commission status, the NESEP and the Hospital Corps. Encourage the Hospital Corps and dental technicians to apply for Medical Service Corps commission status in supply and administration. They weren't getting into that at all, and women had the background for it. It was very good.

Continue to screen enlisted records for qualified enlisted women under the integration program. Continue to publicize the nursing education program. Reemphasize to the field the absolute necessity for quality recruiting. That was particularly true when you have a small number of women, as we did in the Navy. To get quality, you cannot afford to have less than that when your numbers are small.

---

* The basic A School is a level of Navy training that provides specialized instruction that will enable enlisted personnel to strike for a given occupational rating.

Place closer scrutiny on pattern of living, up to enlisted number of changes and locations, and so forth. The necessity for checking records during their academic years—what their professors thought of them, what their high school teachers thought of them.

To follow through and go back to recruit training on cases that were obviously recruiting errors. Point them out to them what was wrong, so they won't do it again. Maybe they didn't check records carefully. That kind of was the most glaring one. They didn't check the individual's records in the community.

Paul Stillwell: Did you have some built-in attrition in recruit training to eliminate people who weren't suitable?

Captain Collins: Yes, academically, that was the big thing. Then we'd find out what recruiting said about them and what the recruit-training command said about them and why they didn't make it and send that right back to recruiting and say, "Look, sharpen up. This is what you're goofing on."

Paul Stillwell: Well, the usual explanation is with the quota staring them in the face, they may lower their standards.

Captain Collins: That's right, yes, that's right.

Paul Stillwell: That's why it was so crucial that you even got the quota put in.

Captain Collins: That's right, absolutely essential. I was going crazy with the recruiting.

Work with the officer in charge, the commanding officer in recruit training in reevaluation of drop-backs at recruit training. Why? Work on the principle that recruits who do not sharpen up should not be sent to active duty. Get rid of them and then go back to recruiting and see why they made that error, but don't send them on.

Encourage outstanding recruit graduates to visit recruiting stations during recruit leave, to attend church social affairs in uniform, to work on making friends in the community. It seems like a small idea, but they didn't think of it themselves. If you encourage them, they do. And at the recruit training graduation, I really got right with them on that point. And of course, it made them proud of their uniform, too, that way.

Improve recruiting aids and techniques. New enlisted mailer, new college junior mailer. Exchange and forming new recruiting ideas and techniques among various recruiting stations. Employe women liaison officers on campuses. Encourage the dissemination of officer training at high school level. Encourage dissemination of work assignments of new reporting ensigns to college students. Have them go back and say what their doing. Develop plans for utilizing reserve officers. Mothers' clubs, ex-WAVES, Navy mothers clubs to assist in overcoming lethargy of public toward women in the Navy.

Encourage better utilization, dissemination of recruiting aids, poster, TV, radio spots, mailers, at the branch and substation level. Keep women in the Navy and before the public and reaching college graduates. Study ways in which reserve officers may be utilized in recruiting.

Then there was a great emphasis on the woman in the Naval Reserve. Quality recruiting again. Monitor performance of administrative personnel connected with these programs. Increase amount of quality recruiting publicity for Naval Reserve division. Ensure that the BuPers leadership team is made available to these divisions.

Paul Stillwell: Well, in a number of cases probably, women completed their time in the Navy enlistment and then got married. What is a motivator to get them into the Naval Reserve?

Captain Collins: Well, that's it. Probably didn't know about it, first of all. So you have to have knowledge of what kinds of billets there were in the Naval Reserve and what you'd be doing and how she could add to her time, her length of service and so forth. And it was just a whole unexplored area, totally.

Paul Stillwell: Well, one of the great selling points for Naval Reserve is the retirement that you qualify for.

Captain Collins: That's right, yes. But if they've been in six, seven, eight years and they get out and don't go in the reserve I think they make a mistake, because they've had almost half time already accumulated.*

Encourage use of women officers on inactive duty as recruiting liaison officers at colleges and universities. This is a very good way to use them to tell about women in the Navy.

Assign additional officers to staff commander Naval Reserve training command. Propose changes in uniform. I told you about that. The new dacron shirts, the new wool slacks, polyester. Elimination of dungarees. New handbags. Modify formal uniform. Emphasize immaculate grooming.

Then great emphasis on naval leadership. And I guess that just about completes me.

Paul Stillwell: Well, you've talked about all these changes. What things did you leave the same? What was working well already?

Captain Collins: Well, recruiting when I left was really good. It was. And morale was greatly improved.

Paul Stillwell: No, I mean what was good when you came so that you didn't have to fix it during your tenure.

Captain Collins: I don't remember.

Paul Stillwell: Well, that's a telling comment.

Captain Collins: I can't recall. It was a bad year that first year. There were so many problems. I just was overpowered by them, really, in so many different kinds of areas: recruiting, discipline, in terms of the self-image, morale, the male attitude toward women. You don't turn it around right away.

---

* At the time, 20 years was the minimum in which to qualify for Navy retirement.

Paul Stillwell: You cannot legislate attitudes.

Captain Collins: No, you can't, but you can really change them. That I know. And I did a tremendous amount of speaking around the country. I tried to visit every command where women were to find out how they felt about everything that was going on in their command. I found some where the commanding officers were impossible. I almost took them away from the naval hospital at Bethesda.* I threatened them. They were working 72 hours a week. Their barracks—the day before I arrived, they put in a TV. They were working all kinds of shifts. They had no place where one shift would have a quiet place to sleep. They just intermingled. I've never seen such a mess. The morale was—well, they were exhausted, frankly. I never will forget talking to the commanding officer. I said, "Unless you improve conditions, you're just not going to get any hospital corps."

He said, "We couldn't do without them."

I said, "You can, because you're treating them like slaves." Imagine, on a regular basis, 72 hours a week. And then not have a quiet place to sleep and no recreation provided for them whatsoever. I just couldn't believe treatment of humans, particularly a medical person. You'd think they'd have some empathy towards a human being more than just a regular officer might.

Paul Stillwell: You're right.

Captain Collins: Because that's their business. No, I really had a real battle with them. And I got them a new barracks, finally. They moved the nurses out and they went in the nurse quarters.

But it's not easy. It's an uphill fight, but a rewarding one, particularly when you accomplish something.

Paul Stillwell: Well, the reward for your accomplishment was that there was nowhere else you could go in the Navy.

---

* National Naval Medical Center in Bethesda, Maryland.

Captain Collins: That's right.

Paul Stillwell: You'd reached the limit of your potential.

Captain Collins: That's right.

Paul Stillwell: Did you retire with a sense of regret?

Captain Collins: Well, no, I'd been married.

Paul Stillwell: When were you married?

Captain Collins: I'd married in '61. My husband was a retired rear admiral.[*] Then the president of Bethlehem Steel wanted him to come up there, so he was commuting from Quincy, Massachusetts, down to Washington. And I was so busy all the time that I just had to devote a tremendous amount of my day and evenings, you know, socially. It was an important part of my job to get acquainted, mingle, be social, and I was very social. And then I did an awful lot of speaking and traveling as head of the WAVES.

Paul Stillwell: When did that come about? Did you get a job shortly after your retirement from the Navy?

Captain Collins: Oh, yes. I did all kinds of things. I became director of an insurance company. I became a consultant to HEW.[†] The Secretary of the Navy asked me to be on his board in which we covered all of the recruits' training and all of the advanced training for enlisted and all the postgraduate school for officers. It was a fascinating job I had then.

---

[*] On 22 April 1961 Captain Quick married Rear Admiral Howard L. Collins, who had retired from active duty on 1 December 1958. He died 3 June 1984, two years before this interview. The two had first met in 1944, when Collins was on the staff of Admiral Chester W. Nimitz, USN.

[†] The Cabinet Department of Health, Education and Welfare, which has since been divided into the Department of Education and the Department of Health and Human Services.

I became the first woman on The Retired Officers Association, the first national vice president of the Navy League. I became a trustee of the foundation, the first woman officer. And then I got this wonderful job as director of CPC.

Paul Stillwell: Well, could you cover the latter in a bit more detail, please?

Captain Collins: Yes. Well, it is an organization of grocery items and sweeteners. They make it from corn, like sweetness for confection, candy, etcetera.

And then in their customers, they have like Skippy's peanut butter, Hellman's mayonnaise, Thomas's English Muffins. Their sales are four billion, six a year. And they're in 47 foreign countries. I was their first woman director. And all my other male directors were presidents of corporations.

I was fascinated with the job, because I'd had two advanced degrees in business administration. And the president said, "If you are free to travel, you just let me know. Because it's like carrying the flag, and in most of these foreign countries they've never met a director." So both my husband and I traveled around the world twice with this corporation, which I thoroughly enjoyed—the same as a Navy inspection. You go in you meet the staff, you talk, you make a speech. Then you go around and meet them. Then they entertain you, keep you up all night, and then you get up early again. But these were very similar to the Navy kinds of inspections, really. But both of us thoroughly enjoyed that. It was a tremendous experience. I was there almost seven years with them.

Paul Stillwell: Well, it sounds as if you kept up with the changes within the Navy too.

Captain Collins: I did, yes, because, the Secretary of the Navy appointed me on that board, of course, I'd had a lot of experience in that area. The other person that was on it was academic dean Bruce Davidson. We first got acquainted when he was at the Naval Academy. We became long-time friends since then. But we traveled all over the country, and I enjoyed that thoroughly.

Paul Stillwell: What have been your reactions to the changes for Navy women since your retirement?

Captain Collins: I wish I'd thought of the white uniform. I don't know why I didn't. I think it's perfect. I wanted to get them in something attractive and I did. And incidentally, the other services, Army and Air Force, adopted something very similar with a different stripe—and the Marines too. They had a green just like that. But I think the white is so attractive, I wish I'd thought of it. I don't know why it never occurred to me. And it's an economical way to go too. It's not separate, then. You get the same material and so forth.

Paul Stillwell: Did you lament the demise of the WAVES as a separate group?

Captain Collins: Oh, no, no, heavens no. That demise happened in '48, you see. People still refer to it as WAVES, and I had to constantly correct my corporation to say, "No, I was not director of the WAVES. I never was. I was Assistant Chief of Naval Personnel. WAVES was a World War II entity, strictly.

Paul Stillwell: But there's no longer a job comparable to the one that you had.

Captain Collins: No, no. Although there is in CNO now. They call it by a different name.[*] They didn't have for a few years, and they got in such trouble, because men just don't react to some of these things the way a woman would—and to stop trouble. And now they have a woman in CNO's office, the Chief of Naval Personnel, there is a woman officer, which makes a lot of sense to me.

Jimmy Holloway called me after I retired, and he said, "Oh, you'd be so pleased with what I've done."[†]

I said, "What?"

---

[*] The director held the position of Assistant Chief of Naval Personnel for Women during the years of 1942-1972. In 1972, the office was disestablished in favor of integration of women into the main force. There still remained, however, the office of Bureau of Personnel Special Assistant for Women's Policy (PERS-00W), which existed until 1991.
[†] Admiral James L. Holloway III, USN, served as Chief of Naval Operations, 29 June 1974 to 1 July 1978.

He said, "I've designed a uniform for active duty women who are pregnant."*

I said, "Oh, no." I said, "Just let them wear civilian clothes. Every mother will think all women are pregnant in the Navy now." He was very disappointed with me. I said, "Ask your wife." And she agreed completely with me, of course.

But that's just a simple idea of a male attitude toward one thing and a woman's attitude. And you just need that little advice, I think, to steer the course carefully.

Paul Stillwell: What is your reaction to women having more sea duty opportunities now?

Captain Collins: I think it's tremendous. Do you want to know my attitude about combat?

Paul Stillwell: Sure.

Captain Collins: Well, one former chief of the Air Force women thinks women should be in combat. I think that women should be in combat if we need them in combat, but I certainly don't think we should push them into combat. I don't think it would make any sense. There are many reasons from a sexual standpoint why the men might be protecting them, or they might have other attitudes of how to use them. I just think it's a crazy idea. I think we'd waste a lot of money, and I have no doubt but what you'd get volunteers, but there are so many problems in connection with it that I would see right off the bat. I'm sure that a man might, but I could point out some others, I guess. And so if we'd ever get to the point in our nation where we had to have women for combat, why then, that'd make sense, wouldn't it? But I don't see that coming.

Paul Stillwell: Captain Quigley said she was disappointed with the trend toward sea duty because many women had joined the Navy because they wanted a career ashore and

---

* Up to 1972, pregnancy meant the automatic termination of a Navy woman's active service. A change that year meant a woman could request to remain on active duty, and in many cases the requests were approved.

didn't necessarily want to go to sea, but they might have to in order to be promoted.*

Captain Collins: I don't think that's a valid excuse whatsoever, absolutely not. Any woman I've talked to that's had sea duty, she loves it. Now, isn't this strange? And I've talked to a lot of them. It's in their career pattern now, and they're very eager to go. No, I don't think they joined that—it is a gradual thing that came about so that those who came in knew that women were going to sea. They got all the great publicity about it, so I don't think that's valid at all.

Paul Stillwell: Okay, so the ones who come in with the new mind-set that that's part of the career, accept it and embrace it.

Captain Collins: Right, yes. I think they're enthusiastic for it. And I've talked to a lot of women at the Naval Academy, and they feel that's part of their career. I mean, so, it's not a problem to them in any sense. I think mostly what is a problem to them is they do not want to be privileged as compared with the men. That is a real morale problem for women. They don't want special treatment, no way.

Paul Stillwell: What might be examples of special treatment?

Captain Collins: Well, let's see. They feel it's right that they should go to sea. I'm speaking of those I talked to at the Naval Academy. They would feel it's wrong if they didn't, because then they would be getting special treatment. They would like an expansion of it for that very reason. I have no doubt that there will be expansion of it. With the numbers of young men diminishing, which is a real problem for all services, they're going to have to put women in more kinds of jobs of that nature, I'm sure. Because they won't have a potential qualified pool.

---

* Captain Robin L. Quigley, USN, served as Assistant Chief of Naval Personnel for Women from 1970 to 1972, when the position was eliminated in that title. Quigley's oral history is in the Naval Institute collection.

Paul Stillwell: I recently met the women's first chief boatswain's mate, which really indicates a change from the old Navy.

Captain Collins: Yes, I'll say. What was she like?

Paul Stillwell: Very feminine, petite, and great satisfaction from her job.

Captain Collins: Oh, wonderful.

Paul Stillwell: She had joined with the thought that she would become an oceanographer, and then once she got the training, she found out that the billet wasn't what was promised. So she dropped out and was sent to a floating dry dock, perhaps as punishment, and saw no opportunity to strike for a clerical rating. So she struck for boatswain's mate and has made it all the way to chief.

Captain Collins: Isn't that something? I think she's probably the only one, isn't she? Chief?

Paul Stillwell: Yes.

Captain Collins: Where is she?

Paul Stillwell: She's at Naval Station Annapolis. She is craft master for one of the YPs that are used to train midshipmen.*

Captain Collins: Well, I'd like to talk to her sometime. That'd be fun.
    Well, I've had a very satisfactory career. I think I told you the only job I had in the Navy but didn't like was when I was in SecDef staff and I didn't have work to do, but fortunately I was selected for Stanford, so I got away. But that was the only job I've ever had in the United States Navy in which I haven't had to work real hard, which I like.

---

* The YP is a yard patrol craft used for training of ship handling and seamanship.

Or most of them I've had, they were innovative and I had to do it. You know, it wasn't done before. And that also appealed to me.

I loved being on the corporation staff. I thoroughly enjoyed it. In fact, I'm going up to New York to a weekend party that the president has invited me to stay at their house. So I keep real close ties. Every year they hold their annual meeting in a different city, and the director and spouse are invited free. And they do things nicely, first class, and limousines and so—that was a new experience. Different from the Navy.

Paul Stillwell: Your service has been a real legacy to the current generation of Navy women.

Captain Collins: Yes, I enjoy talking to them. They like to talk about the kinds of jobs I've had, which have all been very, very interesting and challenging in that they were new, that a woman hadn't been in them.

I was very nervous when I first went on this board and found all these presidents of corporations, and then you're on committees. You're given assignments. And one day the president came up and he said, "Winnie, how'd you like to be chairman of the pension investment fund?" Millions, millions.

I was on the committee, and I found out they were doing very poorly in investments, and I said, "I do better on my own." And I think that got me in trouble. But all of my committee members were presidents of corporations, like Chemical Bank—you know, little—Goodyear, small corporations. But I loved it. And we turned it around.

Mr. Howard McGraw of McGraw-Hill replaced me as chairman. He was on the board—delightful person.

So there are lots of fun factors in every job I've had, as well as a lot of headaches. As you know, this is my biggest headache I ever had in my life, this job, because I felt so many things were wrong.

Paul Stillwell: On the other hand, there are so many opportunities.

Captain Collins: That's right, that's right. I think I went away with a good reputation for women in the Navy, which was one of my goals, definitely, and good morale for them. I wanted them to feel proud of what they were doing and the men to feel proud of them. And I think I achieved that. It's ongoing forever, of course, but it certainly was different from when I took over.

Paul Stillwell: The women who serve now are in that regard your beneficiaries.

Captain Collins: That's right, yes.

Paul Stillwell: And so is the Naval Institute in having you make this contribution to our histories. And I much appreciate that.

Captain Collins: Well, I've been wanting to do this, see, for a long time, but I've had so many interesting jobs after my Navy career, that I've really been very busy.

It's like writing this book. I don't know if it makes sense. I don't know if anybody would want to read it, but it could add a tremendous amount to history of women in our country, I think. And I'll have to talk to you further about going into that, and whether I should or shouldn't and who the publisher would be and so on.*

Paul Stillwell: Okay. Thank you very much.

[Interruption]

Paul Stillwell: You mentioned to me when the recorder wasn't running that you had another situation comparable to the Bethesda one to solve at Patuxent River.†

Captain Collins: Well, this was one of the worst, although I found that often true in inspections. The commanding officer had not thought of the importance of having

---

* The book, *More Than a Uniform*, was published in 1997, two years before Captain Collins's death on 20 May 1999.
† Patuxent River Naval Air Station, Lexington Park, Maryland.

recreation for both men and women. They'd have a bowling alley maybe for the men, but very incomplete kinds of recreation. Young people really like to have a place where they can bring their young women, where they can bring their boyfriends, either in the barracks, which is a recreation, where they have music and they can dance and they can have something to eat. This is a healthy atmosphere, I think.

But I was speaking about Patuxent when I inspected down there the barracks for the enlisted women. They had no place they could go on the base after working hours or weekends. They were surrounded by 24-hour guards who marched around their barracks. The outside community was undesirable for both the young men and young women, very undesirable. I just felt that they were in prison, and I used that term. I said, "You're keeping these people in prison. There's no reason you need to have enlisted women here unless you make changes. And I would think you would want to make changes for the enlisted men the same way. Now, you have many more enlisted men than you have women, so the women must have someplace where they can invite enlisted men. We don't want them en masse. And they need publications for reading, magazines. You can have people come in and talk to them on fashion. You can have special movies and special kinds of programs for them."

I said, "You need some imagination here. Imagine you're a young person, what would you like to do? It's that simple. And talk to some of your young people and find out what they'd like. Talk to some of the women. You've never spoken to them. They said you've never been over there. I want you to go with me and see how they're living." And he did.

Paul Stillwell: This was the commanding officer?

Captain Collins: That's right. I said, "I'll promise you you won't get hit with bricks, but I just want you to see why they have such poor morale."

Paul Stillwell: And he thought he was acting in their interest to protect them from the outside world.

Captain Collins: He was, yes. I said, "They don't need guards. What they need is something to do which is fun. They only work so many hours a day, but look at the kind of leisure time they have in which they have no way to expend their energies, in sports, in meeting boyfriends, in having a little place they could cook something. Those are simple things."

I found the same thing down in Memphis. They had no place for them to go, and no wonder they wanted to get out of the Navy.

Paul Stillwell: Well, inadvertently, he was breaking the promises that your recruiters were making to the women.

Captain Collins: That's right. That's absolutely right, 99.44% men, but they didn't know how to reach them socially. They worked with them, but if there's nothing to do if a command is isolated, and this was isolated. And the community environment was terrible for recreation and in some instances dangerous. So then it's up to a commanding officer to provide that so that his personnel have a variety of activities they can do. It doesn't cost money, it takes imagination is what it takes.

Paul Stillwell: How long did it take to turn around that specific situation?

Captain Collins: Oh, he promised he would. I said, "You won't get another enlisted woman coming in here until you tell me what you've done. And if it isn't done, they're all going to be pulled out."

He says, "You can't do it."

I said, "Test me." I'd have trouble doing it, I'll tell you that. I'd have a lot of complaints all over, but I think I could hold my own on it. But that scared him.

He said, "I don't know what I'd do without them."

I said, "Well, then you'd better treat them like human beings."

Paul Stillwell: It's also likely that were more productive, better workers for having that kind of off-duty environment.

Captain Collins: Of course. How would you and I feel if you had to go and sit in a miserable—they were tenements, I felt, all the barracks. I got most of them converted in my four years to something that they really liked, with a kitchen, a place they could entertain, and two to a room, that kind of thing, which we consider American living. That's our standards. But in the Navy, it was way down here. And when those poor little kids talked to me, I couldn't believe it. I said, "Well, we're just going to change it around. Tell me what you'd like, what kinds of things you want to do."

They said, "We don't want guards."

I said, "That's an easy one. But I want to know what would you want to do in off duty, because the town offers nothing for you." And they said they agreed. They said, "We want a place where maybe we can fix some food, where we can invite a date, maybe some sports outside." You know, things that would create fun and happiness and build morale, really.

So he did it. He got a separate building and he found all kinds of space around, and he really went on it.

Paul Stillwell: Once he got that conversion, he was like a missionary probably.

Captain Collins: Probably. I'm sure, that's right.

So when he saw the barracks—he'd never inspected the barracks. Can you believe it? I said, "This is disgraceful. Here you have this personnel that you rely on so and you can't do without, but you treat them like dirt."

So we had a drink in ending it all happily. Then he wrote me a letter confirming what he was going to do, and he did it.

Paul Stillwell: Did you go back again to see it after that?

Captain Collins: No, I don't think I did, because I didn't have that kind of time, but I did have a woman officer whom I wrote to, with a copy to the commanding officer, saying, "I would appreciate your identifying what has been done in these areas." And so he wrote me, she didn't.

Paul Stillwell: Great.

Captain Collins: But most of it was lack of imagination, really, and some of it was fight, "What can I do with these women? They'll get in trouble." So that's why he had the guards, but he didn't realize he was depressing them so much that they couldn't stand working there. I'm sure their efficiency went down. I mean, you've got to be happy to work.

So that happened time and time again, where there wouldn't be any recreation for them. Air stations, I would say, for the most part were better in imagination, because I think they had a little more money, perhaps, although the training school at Memphis was miserable, absolutely no place for these women to go.

So it was an education for the commanding officers to know that young people require something besides work.

Paul Stillwell: Well, I'm glad we got that one on the record.

Captain Collins: I'll start over then. Captain Victor Smith was head of leadership in BuPers when I was there.[*] And it was a difficult job to define in terms of being a leader for all of the Navy. We became very good friends and one day after the Navy ball—the Navy ball used to be on Monday, why I don't know. But we had our staff meeting at BuPers Tuesday morning. I went around and checked all the eyes to see who had the most bloodshot eyes and the Chaplain, Admiral Rosso, won.[†]

We went in, and we used to call the first chair "Mr. Doom," because that was the comptroller's chair, and we always had just lost so many million every time he spoke. He never brought us any good tidings. And this morning Captain Victor Smith sat in the chair, and Admiral Smedberg said, "Well, I see you've changed your seating arrangements."

---

[*] Captain John Victor Smith, USN. The oral history of Smith, who retired as a vice admiral, is in the Naval Institute collection.
[†] Rear Admiral George A. Rosso, CHC, USN, served as the Navy's Chief of Chaplains from June 1958 to June 1963.

He said, "Yes, because I have a terrible problem in regard to leadership, Admiral. I have puzzled over this, and I don't know how to figure it out. It's very depressing to me. I don't know the answer."

Admiral Smedberg was very serious and he looked at him and he said, "Well, why don't you tell us and maybe, maybe we can come to a solution for you."

So he said, "Well, Admiral, the real point is that I don't know the difference between rape and rapture." He looked at me, and I said, "Leadership."

Admiral Smedberg said, "Did you two get together?"

I said, "No way, it was just an obvious answer for the leadership man." Well, Admiral Smedberg never got over that.

Paul Stillwell: I've heard that story before, and it's great.

Captain Collins: Have you? Well, it's a true story. And Vic Smith always said, "Well, you brought me attention." That's how he got flag rank.

I see him every year when I go out to Coronado. We're very close friends. And I think he's told everybody in Coronado that story.

Paul Stillwell: Well, that's the kind of story that makes a book interesting to read.

Captain Collins: Oh, I'll have to remember that then.[*] See, there's a lot of these that come to me that I didn't include in this, because I had, I guess, a different objective than putting a lot of anecdotes in.

Paul Stillwell: Well, you can do both. They're not mutually exclusive.

---

[*] This anecdote did not make it into her book.

Launched in 1969, the U.S. Naval Institute's award-winning oral history program is among the oldest in the country. Used in combination with documentary sources, oral histories offer a richer understanding of naval history through candid recollections and explanations rarely entered into contemporary records. In addition, they help depict the atmosphere of a particular event or era in a manner not available in official documents.

The nonprofit Naval Institute accomplishes its history projects through contributed funds and gratefully accepts tax-deductible gifts of all sizes for this purpose. This support allows the Institute to preserve the life experiences of today's service men and women so they may enlighten and inspire future generations.

For information about opportunities to underwrite Naval Institute oral history projects, please contact the Naval Institute Foundation at 291 Wood Road, Annapolis, Maryland 21402; by phone at (410) 295-1054; or by e-mail at foundation@usni.org.

Index to the Oral History of
Captain Winifred Quick Collins, U.S. Navy (Retired)

Beardall, Rear Admiral John R., USN (USNA, 1908)
Served as Naval Academy superintendent during World War II, 13

Bethesda, Maryland, Naval Hospital
Substandard living conditions for women stationed at the hospital in the late 1950s, 110

Boone, Admiral Walter F., "Freddie", USN (USNA, 1921)
Served 1956-58 as Commander in Chief U.S. Naval Forces Eastern Atlantic and Mediterranean (CinCNELM), 60, 63-64
Reluctantly joined the Navy League of the United States, 63

Bradley, General of the Army Omar N., USA (USMA, 1915)
Amusing exchanges with Quick when he was Chairman of the Joint Chiefs of Staff in the early 1950s, 30

Bureau of Medicine and Surgery, Washington, D.C.
In the late 1950s revised the height and weight ratios for Navy women, 77

Bureau of Naval Personnel
Developments in the late 1940s as more opportunities opened for Navy women, 35-40
Personnel administration in the early 1950s, 45-50
In 1956 ordered Commander Quick as the first woman officer on the staff of Commander in Chief U.S. Naval Forces Eastern Atlantic and Mediterranean (CinCNELM), 52-53, 57
In the late 1950s enhanced commissioning opportunities for women, 80-83
Assignment of Navy women in the late 1950s-early 1960s, 87-90, 104-105
Humorous byplay between Captain Quick and Captain John Victor Smith in the early 1960s, 122-123

Burke, Admiral Arleigh A., USN (USNA, 1923)
As Chief of Naval Operations, relationship with Captain Quick in the late 1950s-early 1960s, 66, 94

Carney, Rear Admiral Robert B., USN (USNA, 1916)
In 1945 was involved in an amusing case of mistaken identity while serving as chief of staff to Fleet Admiral William F. Halsey, 23-26

Caspari, Lieutenant Commander William J., USN (USNA, 1940)
In the early 1950s assigned personnel to shore duty while serving in the Bureau of Naval Personnel, 46, 57

Cassady, Admiral John H, USN (USNA, 1919)
    Served 1954-56 as Commander in Chief U.S. Naval Forces Eastern Atlantic and Mediterranean (CinCNELM), 60

CinCNELM (Commander in Chief U.S. Naval Forces Eastern Atlantic and Mediterranean)
    Dealings with NATO and other European issues in 1956-57, 56-63

Collins, Rear Admiral Howard L., USN (USNA, 1924)
    First met his future wife, Winifred Quick, in Hawaii, in 1944, 19-22
    Later years with his wife Winifred, 53-54, 111-112

Collins, Captain Winifred Quick, USN (Ret.)
    Parents, 1-4
    Siblings, 3, 11-13
    First husband Roy Quick, 5
    Second husband Howard Collins, 22, 53-54, 111-112
    Youth and education in various states in the 1910s-20s, 1-4
    College experiences in the 1930s at the University of Southern California and at Radcliffe College, 1-8
    Work for Brunswig Drug Company in the 1930s as personnel director, 4-5
    Civilian employment in Southern California, late 1930s-early 1940s, 11-12
    Naval officer training at Smith College in 1942 and service as personnel officer there, 10-11, 14-17
    Assigned 1944-46 as a personnel officer for the 14th Naval District in Hawaii, 17-34
    Duty in the late 1940s for the Potomac River Command and Bureau of Naval Personnel, 31-32, 35-43
    Served on the staff of the Secretary of Defense, 1950-51, 30, 41-43
    Postgraduate student at Stanford University, 1951-52, 43-45
    From 1952 to 1956 served as a personnel officer on the 12th Naval District staff, 45-52
    Served 1956-57 on the staff of Commander in Chief U.S. Naval Forces Eastern Atlantic and Mediterranean (CinCNELM), 56-64
    Served 1957-62 as Assistant Chief of Naval Personnel for Women, 65-111, 118-123
    Post-active duty pursuits, 111-118

Comstock, Ada Louise
    In the late 1930s, as president of Radcliffe College, initiated a small management course taught by Harvard Business School professors, 5-6
    In the early 1940s joined the Secretary of the Navy's Advisory Board for Women in the Navy and recruited Quick, 9

Congress, U.S.
    Involved in the late 1940s in enabling women to serve in the regular Navy, 37-38

Davidson, Dr. Bruce M.
Served 1971-85 as academic dean of the Naval Academy, 53, 112

Disciplinary Problems
For the most part, more Navy men than women got in trouble in the late 1950s-early 1960s, 91, 94, 98

Dougherty, Commander Kathryn, USN
One of the first U.S. Navy women to be promoted to commander, early 1950s, 47, 51

Enlisted Personnel
Hundreds of WAVES were stationed in Hawaii at the end of World War II, 26-29, 33-34
Served on the 12th Naval District staff in the early 1950s, 49
When women were first in the Navy in the 1940s and 1950s, male enlisted personnel were resentful, 55-56
Served in Europe in the mid-1950s, 60-61
Substandard women's barracks in various locations in the late 1950s, 68-69, 92-93, 118-122
Establishment of career patterns and training for enlisted women in the late 1950s-early 1960s, 92-93, 106-107
Female chief boatswain's mate in the 1980s, 116

Fourteenth Naval District, Pearl Harbor, Hawaii
From 1944 to 1946 Quick supervised the duty of WAVES personnel in Hawaii, 17-35

Gates, Thomas S., Jr.
As Secretary of the Navy, relationship with Captain Quick in the late 1950s, 67-69, 91-92

Gravely, Vice Admiral Samuel L., Jr., USN (Ret.)
In his early years as a naval officer, 1940s-1950s, received ill treatment, 56

Great Britain
In the mid-1950s the headquarters for Commander in Chief U.S. Naval Forces Eastern Atlantic and Mediterranean (CinCNELM) were in London, 57-63, 66

Halsey, Fleet Admiral William F., Jr., USN (USNA, 1904)
In 1945, while Commander Third Fleet, had an amusing encounter with three WAVES officers in Hawaii, 23-26

Hancock, Captain Joy Bright, USNR (Mrs. Ralph Ofstie)
Served 1946-53 as Assistant Chief of Naval Personnel for Women, 32, 35, 38-39

Harvard University, Cambridge, Massachusetts
In the late 1930s, Radcliffe College President Ada Louise Comstock initiated a small management course taught by Harvard Business School professors, 5-8

Hawaii
Hundreds of WAVES were stationed in Hawaii at the end of World War II, 17-35

Heald, Captain Wilton S., USN (USNA, 1927)
Served on the 12th Naval District staff in the early 1950s, 49-50

Holloway, Vice Admiral James L., Jr., USN (USNA, 1919)
As Chief of Naval Personnel in 1956, wrote a letter to CinCNELM to say that Commander Quick would be joining the staff, 52-53
Ordered Quick to become Assistant Chief of Naval Personnel for Women in 1957, 63, 70-71

Holloway, Admiral James L. III, USN (Ret.) (USNA, 1943)
As CNO in the mid-1970s approved a uniform for pregnant Navy women, 113-114

Homosexuality
The Office of Naval Intelligence, (ONI) did not correctly interpret relationships among Navy women in the late 1950s, 67-68, 73-74, 89-90

Iacona, Yeoman First Class Mary, USNR
Stationed in Hawaii near the end of World War II to administer WAVES personnel, 27-28

Ingalls, Captain David S., USNR
While commanding the Pearl Harbor Naval Air Station in 1944, arranged housing for WAVES personnel, 27

Lawrence, Midshipman Wendy B., USN (USNA, 1981)
Received the top engineering prize when her class graduated from the Naval Academy in 1981, 53-54

Lockwood, Vice Admiral Charles A., USN (USNA, 1912)
Interaction with Lieutenant Quick while serving as ComSubPac in Hawaii in 1944, 22-23

Love, Lieutenant Winifred, USNR
While serving in Hawaii in 1945, had an amusing encounter with Fleet Admiral William Halsey, 23-26

Mack, Captain William P., USN (USNA, 1937)
In the mid-1950s was a commander detailer in BuPers, 53

Magee, Yeoman First Class Geraldine, USNR
Stationed in Hawaii near the end of World War II to administer WAVES personnel, 27-28

McAfee, Captain Mildred, USNR (Mrs. Douglas Horton)
Served as director of the WAVES in World War II, 11, 15-17, 20, 23, 32

McGirr, Captain William P., USN (USNA, 1925)
Served on the 12th Naval District staff in the early 1950s, 50-5

Naval Academy, Annapolis, Maryland
Restrictions on plebes in the early 1940s, 13
In the early 1960s the Chief of Naval Personnel resisted efforts to assign women officer as academy instructors, 104-105
First classes of female midshipmen in the late 1970s-early 1980s, 53-55

Naval Intelligence, Office of (ONI)
Hinted at homosexual relationships among Navy women in the late 1950s, 67-68, 73-74, 89-90

Naval Reserve, U.S.
Possibilities for Navy women in the 1950s-60s after completing their active service, 108-109

Navy League of the United States
Retired Admiral Walter F. Boone reluctantly became a member, 63-64

News Media
In 1953 the *Christian Science Monitor* published an article on Quick's work with the 12th Naval District, 46-47

Nimitz, Fleet Admiral Chester W., USN (USNA, 1905)
Association with WAVES in Hawaii in 1944-45 and in Washington later, 17-22
Support for Navy women while he was Chief of Naval Operations, 1945-47, 36-38

North Atlantic Treaty Organization (NATO)
In the mid-1950s was involved in status-of-forces agreements with various European nations, 58-60

Nurses
In the late 1950s Navy nurses began receiving orientation training in company with women line officer candidates, 84-86

Patuxent River, Maryland, Naval Air Station
Substandard barracks and recreation opportunities for women in the late 1950s, 118-122

Price, Rear Admiral Walter H., USN (USNA, 1927)
In the mid-1950s served as chief of staff to Commander in Chief U.S. Naval Forces Eastern Atlantic and Mediterranean (CinCNELM), 61-62

Public Affairs
Publicity in the late 1950s-early 1960s to attract qualified women to the Navy, 102-103, 107-108

Radcliffe College, Cambridge, Massachusetts
In the late 1930s, Radcliffe College President Ada Louise Comstock initiated a small management course taught by Harvard Business School professors, 5-8

Recruiting
Efforts to beef up the accession of quality young women into the Navy in the late 1950s-early 1960s, 71-77, 84, 97, 100-101, 107-109

Redden, Captain Lawrence E., USN (Ret.) (USNA, 1946)
Process of getting an appointment to the Naval Academy and as a midshipman in the early 1940s, 11-13

Redman, Rear Admiral John R., USN (USNA, 1919)
Served 1954-57 as Commandant of the 12th Naval District, 46-52

Rodgers, Rear Admiral Bertram J., USN (USNA, 1916)
Served 1950-54 as Commandant of the 12th Naval District, 45-49

Roosevelt, Eleanor
In the 1930s First Lady Roosevelt invited Radcliffe College female business students to visit the White House, 7

Royal Navy
Women reservists in Britain in the mid-1950s, 63

Selection Boards
In the 1950s and 1960s for the promotion of women officers, 47, 51, 82-83

Smedberg, Vice Admiral William R. III, USN (USNA, 1926)
Involved in women's issues while serving as Chief of Naval Personnel in the early 1960s, 80-81, 104-105, 122-123

Smith College, Northampton, Massachusetts
Training for prospective women naval officers during World War II, 10-11, 14-17, 28

Smith, Vice Admiral Harold Page, USN (USNA, 1924)
    Attitude toward Navy women while serving as Chief of Naval Personnel in the late 1950s, 67-70, 78-80

Smith, Captain John Victor, USN (USNA, 1934)
    Humorous byplay with Captain Quick when they were stationed in BuPers in the early 1960s, 122-123

Stanford University, Palo Alto, California
    Navy grad students at in 1951-52, 43-45

Twelfth Naval District, San Francisco
    Personnel issues during the 1952-56 period, 45-50

Towers, Admiral John H., USN (USNA, 1906)
    Served in Hawaii during World War II as Deputy Commander in Chief Pacific Fleet, postwar as CinCPacFlt, 33-35
    Wife Pierrette, 34-35

Tunney, Lieutenant Commander Gene, USNR
    Members of his physical training group briefly taught Navy women to march in 1942, 10

Underwood, Captain Herbert W., USN (Ret.) (USNA, 1910)
    During World War II commanded WAVES officer training at Smith College, 11, 14-17

Uniforms-Naval
    Not initially available for the first women who joined the WAVES in 1942, 10, 14
    Quick's dislike of gray uniforms worn by Navy women in the 1940s and 1950s, 18
    Quick managed to get approval in the late 1950s-early 1960s for a number of changes in the uniforms for Navy women, 78-79, 86-87, 94-95, 99
    In the mid-1970s the Navy adopted a uniform for pregnant women, 113-114

Varian, Captain Donald C., USN (USNA, 1925)
    Served in the Bureau of Naval Personnel, late 1940s-early 1950s, 43

WAVES
    Officer training school at Smith College in 1942, 10-11, 14-17
    Overseas service in Hawaii, 1944-46, 17-35
    Post-World War II demobilization, 31-33

Whitehead, Professor Alfred North Whitehead
    As a member of the Harvard Business School faculty, taught a small group of women students at Radcliffe College in the late 1930s, 5-7

Wilde, Captain Louise, USN
    While serving in Hawaii in 1945, had an amusing encounter with Fleet Admiral William Halsey, 23-26
    Served as Assistant Chief of Naval Personnel for Women, 1953-57, 68-70

Women in the Army
    Status of the WAACs and WACs during World War II, 16

Women in the Navy
    WAVE officer training school at Smith College in World War II, 10-11, 14-17, 28
    The first WAVES officer to marry did so in 1943, 41
    Overseas service in Hawaii, 1944-46, 17-35
    Post-World War II demobilization, 31-33
    Developments in the late 1940s as more opportunities opened for Navy women, 35-41, 65
    Substandard women's barracks in various naval facilities in the late 1950s, 68-69, 110, 118-120
    Developments in the late 1950s-early 1960s as more opportunities opened for Navy women, 71-110
    Pregnancy policy changed in the 1970s, 41, 113-114
    Naval Academy female midshipmen in the 1970s-1980s, 53-55, 115
    Issues related to Navy women in combat, 114-115

WRNS (Women's Royal Naval Service)
    Duty in Great Britain in the mid-1950s, 63, 66

www.ingramcontent.com/pod-product-compliance
Lightning Source LLC
Chambersburg PA
CBHW080611170426
43209CB00007B/1399